The New York

YANKEES

ILLUSTRATED HISTORY

The New York YANKEES

ILLUSTRATED HISTORY

By *Dave Anderson, Murray Chass, Robert Lipsyte, Buster Olney and George Vecsey* **of**
The New York Times

ST. MARTIN'S PRESS ❧ NEW YORK

www.stmartins.com

Book design by Michael Collica

ISBN 0-312-29094-2

First Edition: November 2002

10 9 8 7 6 5 4 3 2 1

Table of CONTENTS

Part One
THE RUTH YEARS
(1903 – 1929)

By George Vecsey

THE GREENHORNS

As hard as it is to imagine, the Yankees have not always been the Yankees.

In this century, the Yankees have been one of the most famous sports teams in the world. The Bronx Bombers generally win the pennant and usually the World Series, too, with only a few lean years here and there. Millions of fans know the Yankees as the franchise of Ruth and Gehrig, DiMaggio and Mantle, Jackson and Jeter. Like many established groups who came from humble beginnings, Yankee fans like to think their team always had pennants flying from Yankee Stadium, that their franchise always had a gigantic flow of cable television bringing in new waves of Mussinas and Giambis to go along with the expensive homegrown talent.

However, almost beyond living memory, there was another team, a marginal team. Second-rate, second-class, second division, secondhand, that itinerant franchise drudged in the shadow of a more glamorous outfit in the very same borough of Manhattan, the New York Giants. The early Yankees, the pre-Yankees, were refugees from Baltimore just trying to hang on in the big city, like many others who have just arrived from somewhere else.

That may be the ultimate triumph of the Yankees—going from refugees to lords of their world, the American Dream, the New York experience. Then and now, New York was a city of immigrants. This role did not begin with the flippant age of David Letterman jokes about taxi drivers who keep chickens in the back seat and must be given directions to Grand Central Station—in Urdu.

New York has classically thrived on exotic newcomers, the Jews and Italians and Irish, the Chinese and Afghans and Nigerians, the woman just off the plane from the Caribbean, the African American man just off a bus from Alabama. In this city of strivers and arrivers, even the mighty New York Yankees came from somewhere else, bringing hope and energy and skill. All this early mediocrity has been obscured since the glorious emergence of a lusty slugger named Babe Ruth and his signature play, the home run. The trademark NY is seen on expensive trademark ball caps all around the world—red ones, green ones, a marketer's triumph. The newest Yankee headgear spreads nearly as fast as news travels on the Internet, but there was a time when they were barely visible in their own city.

Baseball had grown up in urban places like New York; Hoboken, New Jersey; and Cincinnati, Ohio (putting aside the spurious legend of Abner Doubleday's inventing the sport in a quaint upstate village, Cooperstown, New York) and by 1900 had become the national sport, featuring fairly rough characters playing a difficult game on bucolic green lawns in the middle of increasingly large and vertical cities. One of the most accomplished teams was the Baltimore Orioles of the 19th century—forerunners to the current Orioles, the fourth version of that franchise. The original Orioles were managed by John J. McGraw, who was known as Muggsy (for the usual reason people are called Muggsy).

McGraw's Orioles deftly slapped base hits with the leaden baseball of the time, stole bases with sharpened spikes and used their fists as well as their gloves. They dominated the National League in the mid-1890s but then in a business dispute they were disbanded after 1899.

Ban Johnson, the president of the Western League, a man of good reputation and grandiose vision, decided to change the name to the American League, and move a team to New York. In 1901 a new Baltimore Orioles team was formed with McGraw as manager, but it was no secret that this team was headed for the big city. "The American League," Johnson said, "will be the principal organization of the country within a very short time. Mark my prediction."

The established National League was able to hold off the upstarts for two seasons, with considerable help from the Democratic bastion of Tammany Hall, which ruled politics and government and commerce.

Johnson wanted to bring McGraw to New York to manage in his American League, but he and McGraw did not mix well, and McGraw spurned the offer and cast his fate with the Giants. In midsummer of 1902, McGraw moved to New York to manage the Giants for John T. Brush, an enemy of Johnson and of the new league. The Giants also managed to raid the Orioles for several of their best players. The feud was on. Soon afterward, Johnson did move the franchise to New York, not daring to bring the nickname "Orioles" with them because it was much too identified with Baltimore.

New York scarcely blinked. It already had a serious baseball team on the banks of the Harlem River, McGraw's Giants, who would be managed by the cranky little despot from late 1902 through the 1932 season. With baseball the dominant team sport on the expanding continent, the

Giants were the signature sports team of New York, the favorites of the powerful and the plebian alike. Stockbrokers, steel and coal and railroad magnates, politicians, show biz celebrities, all patronized the mid-afternoon games at the Polo Grounds, and so did fans who could barely put together a few nickels.

There was also a team in the borough of Brooklyn, which had just made the huge mistake of being incorporated into New York City, thereby losing its power and independence. The Brooklyn team was known by various nicknames, including Dodgers (short for Trolley-Dodgers, said to be an essential Brooklyn trait) and Bridegrooms and Superbas and Robins (in reference to its avuncular manager, Wilbert Robinson, McGraw's old Baltimore sidekick). Between the powerful Giants and the folksy Dodgers, New York was a National League town, and the ownership of the Giants preferred it remain that way. However, for reasons known mainly to the nefarious leaders of Tammany Hall, the word went out that the second version of the Orioles could now move to New York, with the new owners paying $18,000, a modest sum even a century ago, for the wobbly franchise.

Surely not by coincidence, the new owners—both a bit on the raffish side—had major connections to the crooked empire of Tammany. Frank J. Farrell was known as "The Pool Room King" because he owned a string of gambling casinos, including one on West 33rd Street known as "The House With the Bronze Doors." Farrell also had a stable of racehorses. "He has a fund of good humor and plenty of witty remarks to enliven his conversation," *The New York World* wrote in 1908. "But when in earnest, his jaws come together with a snap. It is then that he has formed his opinion and obstinately clings to it." His partner was William S. Devery, who had gained his stake in the world through the financial opportunities that came to him as chief of police, a major Tammany Hall fiefdom.

With friends in high places, the new owners pulled a swiftie by feinting toward purchasing property near the Polo Grounds. In response, Andrew Freedman, one of the Giants' officials, threatened to run a trolley car line right through the infield of the proposed ballpark. As it turned out, Farrell and Devery really had their collective eye on a property farther to the north, in Washington Heights. It is somehow comforting to know that real-estate shenanigans involving new sports stadiums were going on a full century ago.

Early in 1903 this transient American League franchise made plans to plunk down its new home on a windswept ridge of northwest Manhattan. Nowadays, this ridge is the site of New York Presbyterian Hospital, one of the great medical complexes in the world. The western rooms of the hospital command a sensational view of the George Washington Bridge spanning the Hudson River, as well as the rugged Palisades, the bluffs on the New Jersey side. The majesty of the view and the superb facilities of the hospital undoubtedly help patients get back home again.

The hospital lobby teems with the grand mix of New York—the Hasidic Jews, Dominicans, African Americans, Asians, Muslims, Russians, so many of them from other places, now either seeking medical care or visiting a patient. It is a place of fear and intimidation, but also a place of hope. Directly to the south of this complex, nearly a century ago, three wide city blocks were once inhabited by a hopeful collection of baseball players who were, like many New Yorkers, greenhorns trying to grab a foothold in the big city.

The new owners took control of the team on March 14, 1903, and at noon that day "a dozen wagons were driven into the new American League grounds," according to the *Sporting Life* of March 21, 1903. Home plate would be located near the corner of Fort Washington and 165th Street, which meant right field, backing onto Broadway, was the "sun field." Right-handed hitters faced 168th Street. With the field surveyed, the workers unloaded "wheelbarrows, picks, shovels, steel drills and other paraphernalia nec-

Clark Griffith was manager of the team from 1903 to 1908.

essary for completing the big job on hand," *Sporting Life* added. The park was thrown together in a hurry, a jerry-built collection of planks and pipes, nuts and bolts, with none of the grace and sweep of the oval Polo Grounds a mile or so away.

The unlovely new Hilltop Park rivaled the cold-water flats, the tenement slums in which so many New Yorkers resided. In the earliest dispatches, the team was called merely "New York" or "the Americans," but even before the first game, there were suggestions that it be called the Highlanders, after the general manager, Joseph Gordon, and in tribute to the crack British unit Gordon's Highlanders.

The manager was Clark Griffith, who, in the long sweep of baseball history, eventually became the grand old man of the original Washington Senators. His son moved the Senators to Minnesota in 1961, and four decades later that franchise was in danger of being eliminated as Yankee cable television money crushed its poor competitors. Back then, Griffith was also a regular pitcher—and apparently a would-be fashion designer, too.

"The New York Americans are said to have uniforms that are louder than Bowery hose," wrote the *Sporting Life* of April 25, 1903. "Clark Griffith selected them and his players accuse him of being drugged at the time." Whether induced by hallucinogens or by mere bad taste, the uniforms had a dark blue jersey with large white buttons down the front, and a large white scalloped "N" and "Y" on the front and a blue floppy collar. Psychedelic or not, the uniform was a far cry from the striped majesty of Yankee uniforms a few decades later.

Griffith recruited two players who would

In 1903 Hilltop Park was the new home of the American League franchise located at 168th St. and Broadway.

eventually make the Baseball Hall of Fame— Willie Keeler, a deft hitter known for his slogan, "Hit 'Em Where They Ain't," and Jack Chesbro, an extremely durable pitcher. Then as now, both Manhattan teams trained in the south in March, and reports were sent northward. "A spirit of rivalry will, to be sure, develop, but it will be a helpful one, and not extend to blind partisanship and cut-throat tactics as would have been the inevitable result had peace not been declared," wrote Wm. F. H. Koelsch in the feature "New York Nuggets" in the March 21 issue of *Sporting Life.*

The Americans played their first road game on April 22 in Washington. The locals took advantage of the option and chose to bat first; later the rule was amended to make the home team bat last automatically. Even with last at-bats, the New Yorkers lost their first game, 3–1. A week later, the new park was more or less ready. Sixteen thousand fans waved free flags, the players also waved flags as they marched onto the field and Chesbro proceeded to beat Washington, 6–2. "It was also plain to the critical rooters that the new team is well balanced and shows promise of being able to 'go the route' as they say in the paddock," wrote Koelsch in *Sporting Life.*

Hope springs eternal for fans and maybe even for hometown sportswriters, but the new team did not "go the route." The stands were finished by the first of June and the Highlanders finished fourth in their first year and drew only 211,808 fans in 67 home games, although Keeler batted .318 and Chesbro won 21 and lost 15.

That year there was also a first so-called World Series between the winners of the two leagues, the Pittsburgh Pirates and the Boston Pilgrims. (Some "world": the two leagues did not extend farther west than St. Louis or farther south than Cincinnati or Washington, D.C.) In 1904

McGraw's contempt for Ban Johnson and his league was so great that he refused to play the Pilgrims after the Giants won the National League race. The World Series would resume in 1905, but the new team in New York would not take part for many years.

In 1904 the Highlanders were in contention until the final day. But on October 10, something happened that would seem totally out of character for the Yankees-to-be of later decades and more in fitting with the accident-prone Brooklyn Dodgers of mid-century or the New York Mets of later decades: Chesbro, the talented workhorse, was within one strike of retiring the side in the ninth inning of a tie game. He had a count of two strikes and no balls on the batter, but then went to his "out" pitch, a spitball loaded up with saliva—totally legal in those days—and the ball veered away from the catcher for a wild pitch that allowed the winning run to score. The Highlanders finished a game and a half behind Boston.

To be fair, Chesbro had been busy. He had won two days earlier, and wound up with a 41–12 record in 55 games, a record for victories that will surely never be broken in this age of six-inning starting pitchers and relief specialists. The new team more than doubled its attendance to 438,919 in 75 home games.

After that, the team on the high spine of Manhattan fell into more than a decade of mediocrity—sixth, second, fifth, eighth, fifth, second, sixth, eighth, seventh, sixth, fifth, fourth, sixth and fourth right through 1918.

The Highlanders did have their exciting moments, not all of them wonderful. In 1905, the owners imported Hal Chase, a splendid first baseman with a reputation for gambling. Two of his managers with the team, George Stallings and Frank Chance, would openly accuse Chase of

In 1913 the team was renamed the Yankees and moved in
as tenants to the Polo Grounds.

throwing games. Not only that, but Farrell and Devery started to feud.

Meanwhile, the Giants dominated the city, winning six pennants in the first two decades of the century and usually drawing several hundred thousand more fans per season than the new team. At times, the two teams were forced to get along. In 1910 they actually played a postseason City Series, with the Giants winning four and the Highlanders two. In April of 1911, a fire in the Polo Grounds forced the Giants to play in Hilltop Stadium until June. And on April 21, 1912, the two teams played a benefit for the survivors of the sinking of the *Titanic*.

In 1912 there was the first stirring of the dynasty that would rule baseball. "Highlanders" was too lengthy a nickname to pronounce and fit into headlines, so people began calling them "Yankees," a reference to New Englanders in specific and Americans in general. In 1913, the team

was officially renamed the Yankees, and moved in as tenants to the Polo Grounds. Hilltop Park was razed soon afterward. It took eighty years for the city to get around to placing a plaque that indicated the mighty Yankees had once played there. Meanwhile, Farrell and Devery had drained their stash of gambling and graft money and could no longer afford to hold the team. In January of 1915, they sold the Yankees for $460,000, and both would eventually die nearly penniless.

The new owners were far more substantial. Jacob Ruppert had the wealth of his family brewery and was a three-term Congressman, while Tillinghast L'Hommedieu Huston was an engineer who had fought in Cuba during the Spanish-American War and came home to make his fortune. The two men, introduced by John J. McGraw, of all people, began upgrading their team.

They bought proven players like Wally Pipp from Detroit and Bob Shawkey from Philadelphia,

and talked Frank (Home Run) Baker out of retirement, and the team inched up into the first division. The Yankees did have one major distinction in 1915 although everybody failed to see the importance at the time. On May 6, Jack Warhop of the Yanks gave up a home run to a superb young left-handed pitcher for Boston (now called the Red Sox). In that age of the dead ball and the short, accurate swing, home runs over the fence were a rarity, but this big kid—another greenhorn from Baltimore, for that matter—was strong. It was the first major-league home run for George Herman (Babe) Ruth.

In 1918 the Yankees made a move that would have lasting beneficial effect. With Huston away in the service, Ruppert hired a new manager, Miller Huggins, a former infielder who had managed the St. Louis Cardinals for five seasons. From Europe, Huston lobbied against Huggins, but Ruppert was in control.

As baseball tottered through the last year of the First World War, each team played an abbreviated schedule of 123 games due to travel restrictions. The Yankees were forbidden to play games in New York on Sunday because of the old Blue Laws, and made several forays across the river to Harrison Park in Newark. The Yanks finished third in 1918 and the Red Sox won the World Series for the fifth time in five appearances. Every baseball fan—whether sadistic Yankee fan or masochistic Red Sox fan or just mirthful onlooker—knows the punch line: the Sox would not win another Series for the rest of the twentieth century. One of the pitching stars of the 1918 Series was the very same Babe Ruth. The big kid was now obviously too great a slugger to remain a pitcher.

As the war ended, the Yankees had the aura of

The pitching star of the 1918 World Series was Babe Ruth of the Boston Red Sox.

a perennial also-ran, but this was about to change. On November 1, 1916, there was a propitious event for the Yankees. The new owner of the Red Sox, a New York theater impresario named Harry Frazee, who had bought the team in 1916, needed cash in a hurry.

THE BABE

To this day, Yankee fans deny the concept of Yankee Luck. As far as they can see, the Yankees have always worked hard for the glory that came their way. Those who are less charmed by the dynasty insist that Yankee Luck is some form of arcane magic available to the American League baseball team in New York. The debate dates back to the latter part of the second decade of the 20th century, as the Highlanders-turned-Yankees bumbled along.

One man was about to change all that, and change it forever. He would change it so emphatically that all the other Bronx Bombers could be said to be merely following in his gargantuan footsteps. George Herman Ruth would transform the team, and in the process he would also transform the sport. He was every bit as great an athlete and public phenomenon in his time as Muhammad Ali and Michael Jordan would become later. Even they, in their flamboyant and spectacular ways, followed him. Ruth would solidify what was called the National Pastime and he would create the institution known as the New York Yankees. This franchise, this dynasty, these records (indeed, this book) do not exist without him.

Everybody knows his name. In World War II, enemy soldiers would blaspheme his name across no-man's-land, presuming to insult American sol-

George Herman Ruth would transform the team and the sport.

diers. Many sports fans today know something of Babe Ruth's career, but there is still the danger of missing just how great an athlete he was.

Because the fading photographs and blurry newsreel clippings tend to emphasize the older Babe Ruth, with his big belly and moon face and mincing steps, Ruth has become shorthanded into "the fat guy who hit home runs." You can hear that on sports talk radio from alleged fans (or even born-yesterday hosts) who have never cracked open a record book or history book.

The special quality of Babe Ruth is elusive; you do not have to love the Yankees to love him. Ruth touches even people who grind their teeth as the Yankees win yet another pennant and their ownership behaves arrogantly yet again. Rooting for the Yankees is like rooting for U.S. Steel, goes the old saying. Ruth's mastery matches anything done by the robber barons, the railroad magnates, the steel tycoons (except, of course, he did it fairly and squarely on the playing fields). Therefore he belongs to the White Anglo-Saxon Protestant ideal of America, in that he played hard and he won.

However, Ruth also represents all the outer-borough Roman Catholics and the Lower East Side Jews; a bit on the raw side, not accepted right away. And it is no surprise that his outsider's skills have been adopted by African Americans, some of whom still accept the old and baseless rumor that he was one of them, at least a little bit. Ruth touched all Americans, urban and rural, North and South, schooled and unschooled, in or out. People recognized something of themselves in him, in what he could do, in what they wished they could get away with.

And think about this: All the other Yankee heroes, great as they were, have piggybacked into prominence on the massive accomplishments and charisma of the Babe.

Lou Gehrig can seem remote or Joe DiMaggio haughty or Mickey Mantle surly or Reggie Jackson flamboyant, but they all fit into a Yankee pattern of over-sized greatness that began with Ruth. As imperfect as he was, nothing truly ugly sticks to Ruth, even in a new time of political correctness. When people then or people now refer to Ruth as something of a big slob, they do so with affection—maybe even awe. He was beyond the rules, in ways that almost all public figures, whether politicians or rock stars or athletes, cannot afford to be anymore.

More than half a century after his death in 1948, Ruth's story still inspires a sense of awe. It is almost as if Charles Dickens had created a boyhood so sad, so deprived—so Dickensian—and then turned it over to some modern-day mythmaker: Tiny Tim Cratchit grows up to be Indiana Jones, performing incredible feats of derring-do with a smile on his face.

The long legend of the Yankees begins with this most American of success stories, his childhood of neglect and later raucous excesses, his pitching and slugging, his hamming for the camera and, bringing immense gloom to the new glorious Yankees, his death at the age of 53.

Without Ruth's exploits, this franchise could have become the St. Louis Browns, the Boston Braves, the Philadelphia Athletics: the extra team in town that needed to travel hundreds of miles to seek its own fame. Instead, Ruth brought fame to New York.

He, like the Yankees, began in Baltimore. Because his career became legendary, he inspired legends that were untrue, including the one that he was illegitimate or an orphan. In fact, he was the son of George Herman Ruth and his wife, Kate, whose maiden name was Schamberger. Babe Ruth was born on February 6, 1895, in a family apartment in downtown Baltimore. His parents ran a bar in the neighborhood, only a few blocks from the current Orioles' park at Camden Yards. (During warm summer night games, can the lingering Baltimore spirit of the Babe smell the microbrews and the bratwurst in the stadium's yuppie food courts?)

The Ruths did not seem overtly cruel or mean. They were a young couple with a large extended family. Unfortunately, the young father and the young mother did not have much skill or interest in raising their only son. (Six other Ruth children died in infancy and one daughter lived to be an adult.) By the time he was seven he was running loose in the hard blocks of the waterfront, getting himself in trouble with the police and the courts. On June 13, 1902, George Herman Ruth Sr. signed George Herman Ruth Jr. into the St. Mary's Industrial School for Boys. According to the Babe and others who knew him in those bad childhood days, his parents never visited him at the school, not once.

The boy was among hundreds of youths being kept off the streets and taught to be a tailor or practice some other trade, living in huge dormitories. But this one boy could throw and hit a baseball, and one of the brothers in black robes, a gentle giant named Brother Matthias, recognized the talent as well as the drive. There are old photos of young George Ruth as a left-handed catcher, muscular, lean, intense but also jovial, with a twinkle of a smile. There is nothing mean or lost about him, no bleak orphanage stare. Instead, his hopeful look indicates he enjoys playing this sport, will play all day if they let him, will play for free, and if possible, he will get outside these walls one day soon and play for fame and money, too. He has the healthy look of somebody who means to survive.

When he turned 19 in February of 1914, George Ruth was signed out of St. Mary's into the cus-tody of Jack Dunn, the proprietor of the third version of the Baltimore Orioles, now skulking in the top minor league. The boy was crude in manners and hygiene but wise in the techniques of the pitching mound. In his first training camp in North Carolina, Ruth was dubbed "The Babe" because of his bumptious youthfulness, but the older players could see he was just passing through. By midsummer he had been purchased by the Red Sox.

This is the part of the tale that still stuns even the most knowledgeable baseball fans. We know about the 714 home runs, and how the big guy hit 60 in 1927, two figures that still loom over us, even though they have been surpassed. We know Babe Ruth hit home runs. The statistics are there on page 1421 of *The Baseball Encyclopedia*, amid all the other hitters. However, Ruth's exploits as a pitcher still have the capacity to stun us. There they are on pages 2213–2214 of the very same *Encyclopedia*, amid all the pitchers.

The big kid pitched only four times for the Sox in 1914 and was farmed out to Providence, but he returned in 1915, winning 18 games and losing only 8. In 1916 he had a 23–12 record, and he won his only start in the World Series. In 1917 his record was 24–13. He also hit 9 home runs in the first four seasons, used occasionally as a pinch hitter.

In 1918 some veteran Red Sox players told Sox manager Edward Barrow that Ruth's hitting was too extraordinary to be squandered. That year (flip back to page 1421) Ruth played 59 games in the outfield, another 13 at first, 20 as a pitcher and 3 others as a pinch hitter. He tied for the league lead in homers with 11. But at the same time (flip back to page 2214) he had a 13–7 record as a pitcher, and in the World Series he started two games and won them both.

Ruth still had a 9–5 record for the Red Sox in 1919 but (back to page 1421) he was now playing

H. Harrison Frazee was the owner of the Boston Americans and a New York producer of Broadway musicals. He sold Babe Ruth to the Yankees for $100,000.

the field in 115 games, and he led baseball with a stunning 29 home runs. People went to the games to see him swing, or even miss. They went to see him tip his cap, smile at a child, wink at a woman. He was the biggest thing in the game, yet he had not even reached the team of his destiny.

This is the tale that never ceases to bring tears to eyes of Red Sox fans. The fortunes of the Red Sox (five pennants, five World Series) and the Orioles/Highlanders/Yankees (no pennants whatsoever) were about to intersect. This is where it all began, where it all ended.

H. Harrison (Harry) Frazee, the New York producer of Broadway musicals, owned the Red Sox but felt no particular love or allegiance to them. The history books all agree that Frazee needed money to put on a new musical called "No, No, Nanette!" and he was quite willing to eviscerate his baseball team in order to achieve other ends.

Frazee's first foray into the market came in 1919, when the Yankees paid $40,000 for Carl Mays, a submarine pitcher who had already quit the Red Sox. Then, when Boston did not erupt in civil unrest, Frazee sold other players, too.

Baseball survived the war, playing a short season of 139 games in 1919, but that fall some members of the Chicago White Sox were involved in a gambling plot to throw the Series to the Cincinnati Reds. With those rumors hanging over baseball, Harry Frazee cut a deal with his two New York neighbors, Ruppert and Huston. He needed money; they had money. It was that simple.

On January 3, 1920, Frazee accepted $100,000 for Ruth and another $300,000 in a loan, the collateral being Fenway Park. RED SOX SELL BABE was the top line of the front-page headline in *The Boston Herald*, alongside stories of a Supreme Court decision involving beer, a racy divorce case in Chicago, talk of Calvin Coolidge running for President, and NATION-WIDE SWEEP OF REDS AGAIN BEGUN, about the search for American Communists. The writer of the article about baseball, Ed Cunningham, did his best to present Frazee's side.

"If Frazee is able to obtain players who will place the team in the running by the use of the money he received for Ruth, then the deal may be called a success. Time alone can determine that," Cunningham wrote, never mentioning "No, No, Nanette!" However, two weeks later, when the Yankees moved to buy other players, the *Sporting News* ran another subhead that said: BUY, BUY, BUY IS YANKEE SLOGAN. And it still could be.

Fans and the press had not yet seen the future of rich teams buying players from poor teams, so the transfer of Ruth was still something of a shock. The *Reach Official American League Guide* for 1920 contained a section on "Evil Effects of Star Selling." Its conclusion: "We prefer to believe, however, that the New York Club is just taking one more desperate gamble on pennant honors and World Series pelf." The *Sporting News* of January 15, 1920, ran a story from the Boston point of view that said in a subhead, PROTESTS WILL SOON DIE OUT, MAINLY BECAUSE BABE WAS IN DISFAVOR DUE TO HIS ATTITUDE OVER CONTRACT.

However, two weeks later, the same weekly ran an article from the New York point of view: "Last summer when Ruth was slamming the ball out of the lot with startling regularity, he was lauded by the scribes who are now seeking to belittle him. He was 'Our Own Babe' in Boston in those days, and never was there a hint of the dissension in the club being traceable to him. Now that he has been sold, he is being branded as a troublemaker and a braggart whom Miller Huggins will find exceedingly difficult to handle. Wonder if those scribes who have experienced such a sudden change of heart have ever heard the fable of the fox and the grapes?"

There was some truth to that charge. The big slugger was a handful, and had broken curfew regularly in Boston, although he did recognize the authority of his manager, Ed Barrow. Now Ruth would be managed by spindly Miller Huggins, who had not quite won over the Yankee players in his first two years.

Huggins was the prototypical manager, a former infielder with moderate success who had found his niche as a strategist and ruler of the dugout. In those days before free agency and million-dollar contracts, managers had some control over the conduct of the players, even a notorious playboy like Ruth. Huggins had surely heard about the Babe's lack of discipline, and he rushed out to Los Angeles, where Ruth was spending the winter. After some discussions, Huggins revealed to the New York public that he and Ruth would have no trouble getting along.

Ruth also informed Huggins that he wanted his salary doubled from $10,000 to $20,000. It was a perfect meeting of the minds.

Babe Ruth was now a Yankee. He hit his first New York home run clear over the roof of the Polo Grounds on May 1—against the Red Sox, naturally. For the first time, he was a full-time outfielder, playing in 142 of the Yanks' 154 games, and he dominated baseball as no player had. Ruth hit the amazing total of 54 home runs, drove in 137 runs and scored 148. The Yankees, still a work in transition, finished third again, three games out of first place, but everybody could see they were on their way.

The fans were certainly attracted by the new man. The Yankees' home attendance was 1,289,422, more than double their previous high, achieved the prior season. The Giants shared some of the swag from their tenants, and their own attendance jumped to their own personal high of 929,609, as McGraw's Giants finished seven games behind Wilbert Robinson's Dodgers. 1920 was a seminal year for baseball in many ways, good and bad. In mid-August, Ray Chapman of the Indians was struck in the head by a submarine pitch from Carl Mays of the Yankees. Chapman died the next day, still the only major-league player to die directly from an injury sustained on the field. Then, as the season came to a close, eight Chicago White Sox players were indicted for their roles in a gambling scandal in the previous year's World Series. The players were suspended, and the White Sox faltered in the closing days, sparing the country the spectacle of seeing a team in turmoil performing in the World Series.

The next year saw Judge Kenesaw Mountain Landis installed as the first commissioner of baseball. He and Ruth would be in contact before the year was out.

While Ruppert and Huston continued to bicker, they did agree to hire Ed Barrow as general manager of the Yankees. Barrow made a few good trades and ran a few productive bed checks on Ruth, and in his first season the Yankees became the Yankees. In 1921, the team's 19th season in New York, they finished four and a half games ahead of Cleveland for their first pennant. Ruth hit 59 homers, drove in 171 runs, scored 177 runs and batted .378.

The ball was being juiced to give the fans what they apparently wanted–more offense. The barrage of hitting (five players hit over .360) was supposed to take the fans' minds off the lifetime ban handed down to the eight White Sox players.

The Yankees and Giants then staged the first all–New York World Series, or Subway Series as it came to be known. This was at the end of the experiment with a best-of-nine World Series. The Yankees won three of the first five, but then Ruth came down with an infected arm and sore knee and the Giants won three straight.

Ruth and Landis were soon on intimate terms. Showing signs of the behavior that forsaken Boston sportswriters had predicted, Ruth went off on an illegal barnstorming tour after the Series. Landis scared him off after five games, but also fined Ruth, Bob Meusel, and Bill Piercy their World Series shares—$3,362.26, no small change in those days—and suspended them until May 20 of the 1922 season. Ruth's suspension held down his totals to 35 homers, 94 runs scored, 99 runs batted in and a .315 batting average. But this escapade was only part of his growing legend as an overgrown child who indulged himself in season and out. He had married a 17-year-old waitress at the end of the 1915 season, but he was known as one of the epic carousers of the Roaring Twenties.

Helen Ruth spent most of the year at their huge house in rural Massachusetts while he spent his time in Manhattan, rarely by himself. His appetites were fact and legend to the players, and although the media was hardly as full of gossip and fact as today, the fans got the point.

The players recognized Ruth as a great star who made them some money, and most of them also considered him one of the boys. He had been teased when he was just a year or two out of the reformatory, but he was still lean and rugged enough to scare them with a threat to fight.

Crude bench jockeying was still in fashion in those days before players became trade union colleagues and fellow millionaires. Players would scratch their armpits and make shrieking noises and call him "Ape," and Ruth generally thought that was funny. Major–league baseball was still all white, and some players would insist that Ruth's full lips and broad nose meant he was an African American; Ruth would become enraged and threaten to fight.

Black Americans recognized the left-handed compliment. While banned from playing in the major leagues and generally forced to remain in segregated pavilions behind the outfield, blacks loved baseball and embraced the flamboyance and unique talent of Ruth. Not surprisingly, many blacks incorporated the crude dugout scuttlebutt into urban legend.

It is an interesting myth, but almost surely untrue. Ruth's parents were both of German ancestry; old photographs show his white relatives, many of them looking very much like him. His mother died at age 35, but Ruth's father lived long enough to see his son reach the majors. Ruth obviously had mixed feelings about the parents who had sent him to a reformatory, but he did

Right: By 1921 Babe Ruth hit his 137th home run of his career, surpassing a 19th-century record. He had created a new form of baseball.

visit his father as a major leaguer. Photographs of the two men catch them tending bar in the father's place in Baltimore. The son, barely out of his teens, and the father, barely forty, are clearly father and son.

Ruth contributed to enough legends. The trays of hot dogs; the pitchers of beer; the long line of women visiting his hotel room or his berth on the Pullman cars; the smiles, the kindnesses, the friendship to children. And most of all, the home runs.

By 1921 Ruth hit the 137th home run of his

Ruth was trim and mobile. Despite his thin lower legs and relatively small feet, he could run and had exceptional balance. He was a superb right-fielder who could use his old pitching arm to throw runners out anywhere. And he was a smart player, the way Willie Mays would be decades later. He almost never made a mistake. This is the testimony of his peers, the great players who slashed singles and stole bases and played the game the way it had been taught, but marveled at Ruth's ability to expand the sport.

He could even steal a base—123 in his career, including 50 in his first four years with the Yankees. He had 20 assists from right field in his first season in the angular right field of the Polo Grounds. He knew when to race from first to third on ordinary singles. He was one of the most complete ballplayers ever to play the game.

Babe Ruth knew when to race from first to third on ordinary singles.

career, surpassing the record of a 19th-century player, Roger Connor. He had created a new form of baseball, but he was not a freak, by any means. In his early 20s, before his lack of discipline and normal athletic middle age caught up with him,

In the modern age, most major leaguers swing for the fences and feel no shame whatsoever about striking out. "Part of the job," they say, trudging back to the dugout. Ruth never struck out more than 93 times in a season. Granted, he struck out 1330 times in his career, but he walked 2056 times, which indicates a discipline. And his output of home runs, one for every 11.8 official at-bats, remained the best in history until Mark McGwire retired after 2001 with a ratio of one every 10.6.

Ruth transformed the game, and the Yankees. In 1922 the Yanks beat the St. Louis Browns for the pennant by a game, and once again they lost to the Giants in the World Series. But the tenants of the Polo Grounds had outdrawn the landlords for the third straight season since the Babe came down from Boston. It was time to build a home of their own.

THE STADIUM

By now, Yankee Stadium is generally accepted as America's secular sporting cathedral. In the base-ball temple in the Bronx, the classic speech-teacher tones of Bob Sheppard, the public-address announcer for over half a century, have left echoes worthy of collective choirs, cantors, mul-lahs, and Zen chanters.

Then there is the pantheon behind center field, containing a prodigious assortment of plaques and monuments honoring Yankee heroes who died far too young—Miller Huggins, Lou Gehrig, Babe Ruth, Thurman Munson, Elston Howard, Roger Maris, Billy Martin, Mickey Mantle.

The love and respect for the athletes is also a testimony to the youth and vitality of all those who have played there—the laughing boys of dozens of Bronx summers who snagged hot grounders off the dirt, or unleashed perfect throws from the outfield corners to astute relay men, the relief pitchers who swaggered in from various incarnations of the bullpen, the pinch hit-ters who plunked opposite-field doubles at the appropriate moment, and savored their latest World Championship. And almost from the start, this has been a place where bad things happened to visiting teams.

For all its earthly joys, the tone of the Stadium

Yankee manager Miller Huggins exchanging greetings with Connie Mack, the manager of the Athletics. Huggins, who managed from 1918 to 1929, led the team to six pennants and three World Championships.

remains almost religious: the sweeping depths of the grandstand, the large comfortable enclosure, the boom of the crowds, the echoes, the memo-ries, the fallen heroes. Many fans visiting the Stadium for the first time feel the urge to kneel in awe. This condition also affects visiting players, giving the Yankees an edge. Two mature and per-ceptive players, Tony Gwynn of San Diego in 1998 and Mark Grace of Arizona in 2001, both gushed about the glories of playing a World Series in the Bronx. By the time they had stopped genuflecting, Gwynn's team had lost both games there and Grace's team had lost all three. Do not underestimate the magic dust left behind by Babe and Lou and the rest of them.

The Yankees won their first 26 World Championships in one version or another of Yankee Stadium, whether the early Stadium, the enlarged Stadium or the new reincarnation of 1976. Going into the 21st century, there were major political and economic machinations concerning a new ballpark, to be funded by many millions of taxpayer dollars, but there was one major caveat—that any new stadium somehow retain the haunting majesty of Yankee Stadium.

When Yankee Stadium opened in 1923, everybody acknowledged it would not have existed had it not been for the lusty slugger from Baltimore and Boston. The Babe had set the steam shovels in motion.

He hit only a few home runs as a Yankee before the haughty Giants realized that their landlord-tenant relationship had gone askew. By May 14, 1920, the Giants' owner, Charles Stoneham, and the surly manager, John McGraw, announced that the Yankees could no longer share the Polo Grounds. They suggested that two stadiums would benefit both teams, since they could schedule more Sunday games, but in reality that was not how the major-league schedules worked, then or now. It was only an excuse to get the Babe out of the Giants' home.

McGraw, the old Oriole, even tossed barbs that Ruth was nothing more than a one-trick pony who could not get away with his swing-from-the-butt shenanigans in the "real" league, the National League. This was pure hyperbole, bordering on jealousy, and everybody could see it. The Yankees had purchased another breed of giant who was changing the balance of power in New York.

The two owners of the Yankees did not need any signals from the Giants to know that a new stadium was in order. They had been thinking of their own palace since purchasing the Yankees from the tapped-out Farrell and Devery in 1915. Now, with Ruth putting the ball over the fences, Ruppert and Huston could talk terms with architects and builders.

Starting in September of 1920, the Yankee owners began looking at the Hebrew Orphan Asylum property at 135th Street and Amsterdam Avenue in Manhattan, just a mile south of the Polo Grounds. But eventually they discovered a better site across the Macombs Dam Bridge spanning the Harlem River, and they paid $600,000 for a sawmill belonging to William Waldorf Astor. The beauty of the area was that it would be served by the subway. There was even talk of building a railroad station alongside existing lines only a few hundred feet to the west of the proposed ballpark, to make it easier to reach from the northern suburbs as well as midtown. Incredibly, in a city that brags of its urbanity and foresightedness, that station was still yet to be built by 2002 as planners debated the future of the Yankees in the Bronx.

Back in 1920 Ruppert, with his old money, and Huston, with his somewhat newer money, had grandiose plans. They wanted a ballpark that would be worthy of the name "stadium," a word never before attached to a baseball field. To prove how serious they were, the owners went outside their local Tammany connections, no popular step, one can assume. They brought in the Osborne Engineering Co. of Cleveland, which on February 6, 1921, began surveying the land that sloped down from the rocky Bronx hills toward the shore of the Harlem River. They planned a huge structure that would loom impressively across the river at the Polo Grounds.

Yankee Stadium was completed in 284 days by the
White Construction Co. of New York.

The Polo Grounds had been designed by necessity (not for polo, either; that sport was never once played there), since it occupied a relatively narrow plot tucked in below the looming rocks of Coogan's Bluff. The Polo Grounds had to have short foul lines and overhanging decks in left and right field, much to the confusion of pitchers and hitters who tried to alter their games in that odd place. But Yankee Stadium, with all that open space around it, was designed to facilitate the new postwar thrill, the home run. Babe Ruth hardly needed help on most of his shots, launched on an upward trajectory, but he had also gained from wicked pulled line drives down the short right-field line in the Polo Grounds, and Yankee management wanted to duplicate the short porch in the Bronx.

So the dimensions were set at 280 feet down the left-field line, followed by a long deepening angle toward left-center field that would soon be called Death Valley, where right-handed hitters saw their best shots simply die of exhaustion. Center field was a formidable 490 feet. And then right field sloped back to a very cozy 295, a little boost for the Bambino. The stands ended before the foul lines on both sides, so Ruth would be aiming his shots at low-slung bleachers and open sky.

Some sportswriters labeled the dimensions a farce. But Fred Lieb, a leading sportswriter for *The New York Evening Telegram*, got it right. He called the new place "The House That Ruth Built." On May 6, 1922, the White Construction Co. of New York began work. It was a Saturday, and workers did not receive overtime in those days. The official count from start to completion was 284 working days, and the stadium was ready for the first day of the 1923 season, at a cost of $2.3 million.

People then as now referred to Yankee Stadium as a "triple-decker," but the architects and builders and owners noted that was technically not true. "They insist that the stadium, something entirely new in grandstand construction, is a double-decker plus a mezzanine," said the *Reach Official American League Guide* for 1924. "A triple-decker would have required a much greater height, which should have been prohibitory."

It was a fine point, worth remembering, just as the current Yankee uniforms are, technically, not pinstriped because that phrase implies a fine line of dots, whereas the Yankee stripes are continuous lines. I have a journalist friend who badgers me (from Dublin, Ireland, no less) whenever somebody refers to the "pinstriped Yankees."

At any rate, the Stadium was huge, impressive

Left: Yankee Stadium opened on April 18, 1923.

and, most important, ready for action on opening day. It was cold and blustery the day they opened it, April 18, 1923, but the fans packed the place. Photos of the day show the elegant top-hatted, topcoated downtown crowd, with attendant

Officially, 74,217 fans packed the new facility on Day One.

black sedans and limousines lined up outside. From the first day, Yankee Stadium was "king of the hill, top of the heap," as the song "New York, New York" would proclaim about the city itself many decades later.

"The new $2,500,000 Yankee Stadium is almost half again as large in capacity for spectators as the ancient Colosseum of Rome," wrote Raymond C. Carrroll of *The Philadelphia Ledger*. "It is a thrilling thought that perhaps 2,500 years from now, archaeologists, spading up the ruins of Harlem and the lower Bronx, will find arenas that

The Yankees meeting Commissioner Judge Landis,
with cane, on that inaugural day.

outsize anything that the ancient Romans and Greeks built."

Carroll then noted the estimates of an opening-day attendance of 74,217 was more likely 60,000 fans inside and the rest outside. He compared the possible exaggeration with the claims of 87,000 people in the old Roman Colosseum, saying that the famous historians of Rome, Pliny the Elder and Pliny the Younger—uncle and nephew—as well as Herodotus from Greece, "thought nothing of adding a cipher or more to an estimate; they were careless reporters, indeed, and may have been out-and-out fakers." Carroll was one of the first to remind us that myth and legend and embellishment are part of the Ruthian legacy.

Most details of the Ruth era are indisputable, to be sure. The American League schedule-maker did not miss a chance for delicious irony, sum-

It was a packed house as the Yankees played their first World Series
game at Yankee Stadium on October 10, 1923.

moning the Boston Red Sox to be the first oppo-
nent. Not only that, but Harry Frazee himself
showed up for the big day, no logistical big deal
since his show biz offices were in Times Square.
Wearing an elegant topcoat with a black bow tie
visible, Frazee is seen in old photographs smiling
and strutting near the new commissioner, the
white-thatched Judge Landis.

Frazee had every reason to be happy. He had

sold the Yankees a large chunk of their productive
players. The occasion seemed like a family
reunion. Red-white-and-blue bunting was hung
from the upper deck, the mezzanine and the railing
surrounding the field. Governor Alfred E. Smith,
with his classic "berled-in-erl" New York accent,
was there, but Mayor John F. Hyland had to miss
the game because of the flu. Manager Huggins
hoisted the flag in deep center field and the

Seventh Regiment Band, conducted by John Philip Sousa himself, played the "Star-Spangled Banner," which was not yet a daily ritual at sporting events, but reserved only for major happenings.

That first day turned out the way so many future days would turn out. The Yankees drubbed their victim by a score of 4–1, the margin coming from a three-run homer by Ruth, which rocketed into the area already known as Ruthville.

"The moment Ruth's drive landed among the bleacher spectators, the crowd went mad. Hats, canes and umbrellas were thrown up and a tremendous volley of cheers greeted the smiling Bambino as he trotted around the circuit," reported *Sporting News* a few days later.

"Ruth needed just such an outburst of joy to swell his chest with pride," the weekly continued. "He had been in the dumps as a result of rather feeble hitting on the training trip and evidently was growing nervous. So when he jumped the old apple into the yawning and conveniently located stand for a job around the bases he found himself a hero once more and was happy."

Ruth's home run assured him and Yankee fans that all the new power and skill had been successfully transferred from Manhattan to the Bronx.

Soon after the opening game, there was a major change in the affairs of the Yankees. Ruppert and Huston, always an odd couple, had grown increasingly estranged after Ruppert hired Miller Huggins while Huston was away at war. The gap widened when Huston and his star player, Ruth, began running around together, sampling the city's many temptations. On May 21, 1923, Ruppert bought out Huston for an estimated $1.25 million. Ed Barrow purchased 10 percent of the team for $300,000.

The first game in the new Stadium turned out to be a preview of the season. During a midwin-

ter banquet, Ruth had been publicly taunted by Jimmy Walker, the hard-drinking, skirt-chasing state senator and future mayor, into cutting down on the carousing. The challenge was so blunt that Ruth blubbered on the dais and promised to reform. That year, he did, hitting 41 homers and driving in 130 runs with a .393 batting average, the highest of his career. The Yankees won 98 games, tying their record of 1921, and they won the pennant by a stunning sixteen games. Oddly enough their attendance dropped to 1,007,066, below the three years they had played with Ruth in the Polo Grounds, but at least the Yankees were not paying rent anymore. (The Giants' attendance dropped even more drastically, to 820,780.)

Both teams received World Series receipts. The Yankees took on the Giants in the first New York series involving two ballparks—and within view of each other. They alternated home games, a rarity even in intracity World Series.

The Series began on October 10, 1923, in Yankee Stadium, but the honor of the first World Series homer in Ruth's House belonged to an itinerant outfielder for the Giants named Charles Dillon Stengel. Known for his pranks and his strong will, Casey—he was from Kansas City—Stengel had been around the National League. In the first game, Casey drove a pitch between two fielders in deepest Death Valley. As he rounded second base, Stengel slowed down, possibly because his shoe had become loose or possibly because of his advanced 31 years. Lumbering around third, he slid home just ahead of the throw for an inside-the-park home run.

Many years later, Stengel would manage the Yankees from 1949 through 1960, winning ten pennants, and after that he would manage the dreadful expansion franchise, the New York Mets out in Queens, from 1962 through 1965, winning

Joe Bush, touching home plate, and Whitey Witt score on Joe Dugan's homer in Game 5 of the 1923 World Series at Yankee Stadium. The series would go six games as the Yankees would win their first World Championship.

no pennants and not that many games, either. Having played for the Dodgers and Giants and managed the Mets and Yanks, the Old Professor is probably the quintessential New York baseball man. For the half–century of their marriage, Casey delighted in telling how Edna Lawson's family, witnessing the old geezer stumbling his way home, said she'd better marry him before he died of old age.

After Casey helped the Giants win the first game, Ruth hit two homers in the second game, as the Yankees won. The irrepressible Stengel hit a seventh-inning homer for a 1–0 Giant victory in the third game—and thumbed his nose at the Yankee dugout as he passed third base. He could get away with it, since he hit .417 in that Series. Then the Yankees won the fourth, fifth and sixth games for their first World Championship. Ruth finished with three bases-empty homers, eight walks, eight runs scored and a .368 average. The high average was by the Yankees' second baseman, Aaron Ward, who hit .417 and began a tradition of World Series heroics by Yankee second basemen (Bobby Richardson, Brian Doyle, Luis Sojo, et al.).

The Yankees now had baseball's greatest star, baseball's greatest stadium and their first World Championship. They were on their way.

David Atkatz, a physics professor at Skidmore College in New York (and an unofficial Yankee historian), was born within sight of Yankee Stadium. His collection of Yankee memorabilia, from which these examples have been selected, emphasizes the first quarter-century of Yankee history.

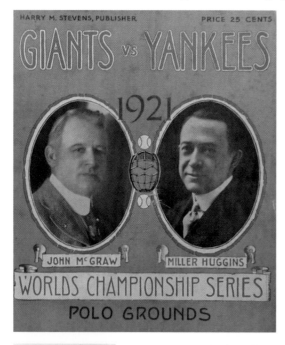

The Yankees' first World Series game, October 5, 1921. Left and above: Souvenir program and ticket stub. Below left: Baseball signed by the Yankee battery, Carl Mays and Wally Schang.

Left: The original holder of this ticket cried along with Lou Gehrig on July 4, 1939, as "the luckiest man on the face of the earth" bade his fans farewell.

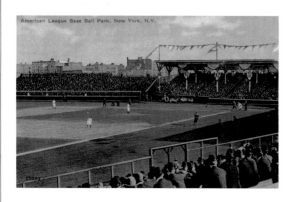

Left: The Yankees' first home, Hilltop Park, circa 1910. Above: Baseball signed by the "Greatest of All," the fabled 1927 team.

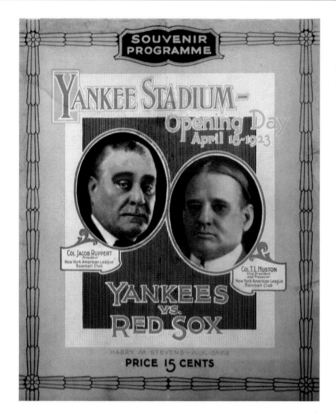

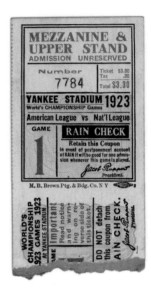

Some Yankee Stadium "firsts": (Clockwise from left) Program from the first game played in the "House That Ruth Built." Rain check from an engraved invitation to that game. Ticket stub from the Stadium's first World Series game, October 10, 1923 (the N.Y. Giants won on Casey Stengel's inside-the-park home run).

Program from the inaugural season of 1903, picturing Highlander skipper Clark Griffith.

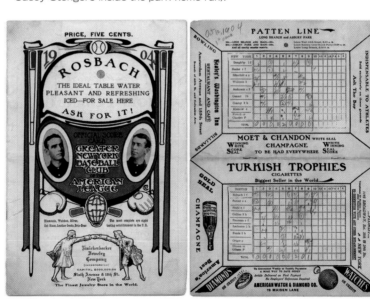

The Yankee–Red Sox rivalry begins here. On the last day of the 1904 season, with the A.L. flag in the balance, New York's ace Jack Chesbro's wild pitch sent the pennant to Boston. This filled-in scorecard, with Griffith and Willie Keeler pictured, may be the only one surviving from that game.

THE DYNASTY

All the wheels were in motion for Yankee domination in perpetuity. On the very afternoon that Yankee Stadium opened, a young left-handed pitcher for Columbia University struck out 17 batters from Williams College in a game played on the Columbia campus. That young lefty was Lou Gehrig, and he sometimes played first base because, like Babe Ruth, he could also hit a little.

On another afternoon that spring, Paul Krichell, the Yankees' eastern scout, witnessed Gehrig slugging a home run that bounced on the high steps of Low Library, 500 feet away. That field is long since gone, replaced by a quadrangle where Frisbee is now the game of choice. But the steps to the library remain, and one stroller in a thousand may connect them with the fabled hero of the Yankees. "I knew then that I'd never have another moment like it the rest of my life," Krichell would say over the years.

Henry Louis Gehrig was a New Yorker, born on June 19, 1903, in the Yorkville neighborhood, home to German immigrants such as his parents. Later the family moved to West 170th Street and Amsterdam Avenue, not far from the disappeared Hilltop Park. Now grown to a burly six feet, 200 pounds, Gehrig was attracted to the Yankees as his hometown team, which Ed Barrow undoubtedly manipulated to the Yankees' advantage when talking contract.

Edward Grant Barrow was always pushing. After managing Ruth in Boston, he came to the Yankees as general manager, still believing that if a man could hit .350 or so while swinging for the fences, he could do even better if he concentrated on making contact. Fortunately, Ruth was beyond that kind of pressure, but he did call

Lou Gehrig would have 493 homers and a .340 batting average with the team.

Lou Gehrig played in 2,130 consecutive games for the team.

Barrow "Manager" and apologize abjectly whenever he went too far. Barrow was devoid of humor, and was not embarrassed by his cold and brutal negotiations with players. He did not want to be their friend. And he kept prodding at the weaker teams in the league to see what he could pry loose.

For his first season in 1921, Barrow made a rather one-sided trade with the Red Sox, importing four useful players, including catcher Wally Schang and pitcher Waite Hoyt. In July of 1922, Barrow brought in Joe Dugan from Boston to play third base. Also in 1922, the Yankees got Joe Bush, Sam Jones and Everett Scott in trades. Then in 1923 Barrow brought in Herb Pennock, a patrician pitcher from Boston who was respected by the Babe.

They were so flush that they could afford to stockpile the powerful young man off the Columbia campus. Gehrig served his apprenticeship in 1923 and 1924, appearing in only 23 games as the Yankees sputtered and finished second. In

1925, Ruth was taken off a train during spring training, suffering from an illness that was alleged to be a stomachache, but may have been some form of venereal disease that needed immediate surgery. At any rate, Ruth missed April and then he missed May, and the Yankees were stumbling along in the second division.

On June 1, Ruth came back, weak but available. Late in the game, Gehrig pinch-hit for Pee Wee Wanninger, the shortstop. The next day, Wally Pipp, the regular first baseman, still only 32, came down with a headache and needed a day off. Although he did not know it at the time, Pipp was about to become a famous name in sports history. Whenever any American athlete feels inclined to take a day off, he or she probably thinks of the words "Wally" and "Pipp." Gehrig started that day, and would start the next 2,128 consecutively. He batted .295 with 21 homers the rest of the season and Pipp was sold to Cincinnati.

That was just the beginning for the man they

Lou Gehrig having fun with Babe Ruth. The two
were teammates for 11 years.

called the Iron Horse. Gehrig would finish his
career with 493 homers and a batting average of
.340. Once he hit four home runs in a game. But
this statistic blows the minds of every generation
that never saw Henry Louis Gehrig play: With
legs that could support the front end of a freight
engine, Gehrig stole home 15 times in his career
out of a respectable total of 102 stolen bases.
Gehrig's fifteen steals of home is one of the great

statistics in baseball, along with Joe DiMaggio's
amazing ratio of only 369 strikeouts to a power-
hitter's career of 361 homers. But Gehrig's muscles were also impressive.

"Lou hit four line drives one day," Tommy
Henrich once recalled of his rookie year. "I'd never
seen line drives like that before. But when I mentioned it to Bill Dickey, he said, 'You only saw soft
line drives. Wait until you see his hard line drives.'"

Babe Ruth watching his 60th homer on September 30, 1927.

The 1927 Yankee infield, from left, Lou Gehrig, first base, Tony Lazzeri, second base, Mark Koenig, shortstop and Jumpin' Joe Dugan, their third baseman.

The line drives were no accident. When Ruth and Gehrig were occasionally photographed shirtless, the viewer probably noticed Ruth's mobile expressions before observing the sculpted muscles of Gehrig.

Ruth's theatricality paid off for him at contract time. While Ruth's peak salary was $80,000 a year, Gehrig labored at half that wage. In the Gehrig biography "Iron Horse," author Ray Robinson recalls how the players felt Barrow was getting Gehrig cheaply because of his loyalty to the team and his hometown.

"It's too bad that Gehrig is so underpaid," Joe DiMaggio said in 1936.

Ultimately, Gehrig would be named the first captain of the Yankees.

"By nature Lou was a serious person, quite caught up in his self-designated role as loyal son, loyal team player, loyal citizen, loyal employee," Robinson once wrote. Gehrig established himself

The 1927 Yankee pitching staff, from left, Bob Shawkey, Joe Giard, Myles Thomas, Urban Shocker, Waite Hoyt, Herb Pennock, Wilcy Moore, Walter Beall, Dutch Ruether and George Pipgras.

in 1925 as the Yankees staggered home in seventh place. It was not always easy to be Miller Huggins, the scrawny and sick manager. Ruth sniped at him, Sammy Vick punched him and Huston had resented him, but Huggins endured, partially because Gehrig was such a solid citizen.

They got back in gear in 1926, winning the pennant but losing to the St. Louis Cardinals in the World Series. The next year, the Yankees achieved one of the greatest seasons of any baseball team in history. Ruth broke his own record with 60 homers, and Gehrig added 47, leading the league in runs batted in with 175. In a decade when gangsters had a lot more panache than they do today, the Yankees were called "Murderers' Row," and not just because of Ruth and Gehrig, either.

At second base was Tony Lazzeri, a quiet Hall of Fame player who hit .309 and drove in 102 runs. At third base was Jumpin' Joe Dugan. At shortstop was Mark Koenig. In left field was Bob Meusel, who batted .337 and drove in 103 runs. In center was fleet Earle Combs out of Kentucky. The catching of Pat Collins and Johnny Grabowsky was undistinguished, but the pitching was superb—Waite Hoyt, George Pipgras, Herb Pennock, Bob Shawkey and Wilcy Moore, one of the first relief pitchers in history.

Yankee legends are so numerous that one has to pick and choose, but this one is unavoidable: The Pirates had won their own pennant over the Cardinals, paced by the Waner Brothers, Paul (Big Poison) who batted .380 and Lloyd (Little Poison) who batted .355. They were no slouches, but they had been reading the box scores all season, and they knew the numbers the Yankees had put up.

In those days there was no television, which meant no daily highlights on the 11 o'clock news, no blur of home runs soaring over fences, which seems to be the sum of knowledge that news producers have about baseball. The Pirates might see photos of the Bombers, or catch a rudimentary newsreel, but there had been no opportunity to watch the Yankees.

So on the eve of the World Series, when the Yankees traveled out to Pittsburgh to take batting practice in spacious Forbes Field, on the campus of the University of Pittsburgh, legend has it that the Pirate players stood around and gaped. Maybe they didn't gape. Maybe they just watched. Maybe Big Poison and Little Poison actually chatted collegially with their brethren in the home uniforms, although fraternization was not common in those days. At any rate, the myth is that the Pirates gaped. And then they gaped some more in the four games that ensued. The Yankees won 'em all, 5–4 and 6–2 in Pittsburgh and 8–1 and 4–3 in the Stadium.

In 1928 the stands were extended in left and right field, giving Yankee Stadium an even more awesome enclosed feeling, and raising attendance. In the 1928 World Series the Yanks beat the Cardinals in four straight games but then went three years without winning a championship.

In 1929 the Yankees became the first team to wear numbers, starting logically with the regular batting order, which meant that Ruth was No. 3

Joe McCarthy became the team's manager in 1931. He managed the team to eight championships and seven World Championships.

Image on following page: Babe Ruth is congratulated by Lou Gehrig after Ruth hit a homer in the fifth inning of Game 3 of the 1932 World Series in Chicago against the Cubs. The debate continues whether or not Ruth called this homer.

and Gehrig was No. 4. The catcher was Bill Dickey, No. 8, a future Hall of Famer in his first year as a regular. Toward the end of that season, Huggins died at the age of 50, from an inflammation of the skin. Three years later, on May 30, 1932, the first memorial in Yankee Stadium's center field was dedicated to the intense little manager, beginning the powerful blend of glory and mourning in the Stadium.

In 1930 the Yankees made Bob Shawkey the manager. Early in the season Barrow brought in Red Ruffing, a powerful pitcher who could also hit, from his old stomping grounds of Boston. Ruffing went 15–5, but the Yankees finished third.

Babe Ruth chopping some wood on his farm.

After his first season as manager, Shawkey was not amused to walk into a press conference introducing Joe McCarthy as his successor for 1931. A former manager of the Cubs, McCarthy was as stern as Barrow, doing away with the card table, installing a dress code and prohibiting shaving in the clubhouse, saying that players were expected to report for work clean shaven. Ruth resented McCarthy because the Babe had managing aspirations of his own.

The Yanks finished second in 1931 during the worsening Depression, Barrow whacked $5,000 off

Ruth's peak salary of $80,000, and the team regrouped, winning 107 games in 1932. The highlight of that season was the World Series, with the Yankees taunting the Cubs as cheapskates for awarding only half a share of the Series loot to their old teammate, Mark Koenig, now with the Cubs.

Ruth hit a home run early in the third game. Later, he made a gesture with his right hand while waiting for Charlie Root's next pitch. Ruth promptly clouted a home run into the center-field bleachers, prompting a debate that still rages. Did he call his shot, or didn't he? To their dying

Babe Ruth played Santa Claus at a children's charity event
at the Hotel Astor in New York in 1947.

days, the Cub players insisted Ruth had not predicted a homer. Many Yankee players said he did.
Most of the reports of the game did not indicate
he did, although John Drebinger of *The New York
Times*, hardly a sensationalist, was one of the few
to say he did. Given the rudimentary slowness of
cameras of that time, the images are inconclu-
sive. Some photographs show Ruth extending his
hand but his gesture seems more toward the
mound than the bleachers. Nevertheless, it was
yet another legend involving the Babe.

Even with all his home runs and education and

his impeccable behavior, Gehrig, No. 4, was
always one step behind Ruth, No. 3. Gehrig was
often photographed standing around politely
while Ruth chatted with fans, posing with any hat
handed to him—military, sporting, cowboy,
derby, ball cap.

The Yanks finished second in 1933, 1934 and
1935, gaining McCarthy the nickname of Second-
Place Joe. By then Ruth realized he was not going
to oust McCarthy as manager, and went over to
play for the Boston Braves for a few months. He
even hit three homers in one game in Pittsburgh,

The bleachers are packed on July 4, 1939, the day Lou Gehrig offically retired.

"Today I consider myself the luckiest man on the face of the earth," said
Lou Gehrig in a moving farewell speech.

a few days before retiring, and later he coached in Brooklyn, but he knew he was just being used for publicity.

Ruth, long remarried to Claire Hodgson, had settled down in his own fashion, and was a loving father of two adopted daughters. A few years ago, Hofstra University held an academic conference on Babe Ruth, and invited Julia Ruth Stevens, who, in an interview, talked lovingly of her adoptive father. "I don't know about Daddy's life before he married my mother," Mrs. Stevens said,

"but I just know he was home a lot of the time, and he was a very good husband and father."

The man with such a bleak childhood often brought Julia with him on public appearances, and seemed to glow at having a family. He lived as a celebrity on the Upper West Side of New York, a good-hearted version of the Duke of Windsor, a royal with no throne, giving his time to charity, visiting children and waiting for somebody to make him a manager, which would never happen, and perhaps he knew it.

Gehrig and his wife, Eleanor, would never have a family. In the spring of 1939, Gehrig found himself inexplicably clumsy and on May 1 he took himself out of the lineup. He was soon diag-

Image on preceding pages: Lou Gehrig decides to take himself out of the lineup on May 1, 1939, after playing in 2,130 consecutive games. He watched his teamates work out before their game against the Tigers in Detroit.

Babe Ruth showed up at Lou Gehrig's farewell and threw his arms around Gehrig's neck.

nosed as having amyotrophic lateral sclerosis, a rare and incurable nerve disease.

Two months later, on July 4, 1939, between games of a doubleheader in Yankee Stadium, he officially retired in a moving ceremony at Yankee Stadium, declaring, "Today I consider myself the luckiest man on the face of the Earth." That speech, recited by Gary Cooper in the movie "Pride of the Yankees," is exactly as Gehrig wrote it. Most amazingly, the screenwriters did not try to tamper with what the earnest Columbia man had put down on paper.

Ruth and Gehrig had not been friendly since Gehrig's mother had been overheard criticizing Ruth's wife during a communal vacation in 1934.

However, the Babe showed up at Gehrig's farewell and threw his arms around Gehrig's neck and blubbered his heart out. Kindly Ed Barrow was heard to say it was time for Gehrig to find another line of work. To make sure he did, Barrow cut off Gehrig's salary, too. After all, the man couldn't hit anymore.

Organized baseball was a little kinder. Gehrig was installed in the new Hall of Fame in Cooperstown in 1939, after officials waived the mandatory five-year waiting period.

Gehrig died on June 2, 1941, only sixteen years to the day after replacing Wally Pipp. He was not yet 38. Today, the disease that killed him is generally called Lou Gehrig's Disease, a grim legacy for anyone. After he died, the Yankees placed a monument to him in deep center field, adding to the pantheon of departed heroes.

Soon there was another memorial. Ruth, always a heavy smoker, came down with cancer after World War II. There are familiar film clips of his farewell appearance in Yankee Stadium on June 13, 1947, in front of 58,339 fans.

Wearing a heavy camel's hair coat to protect him against the chill of impending mortality, Ruth delivered a short rambling talk that began: "Thank you very much, ladies and gentlemen. You know how bad my voice sounds. Well, it feels just as bad. . . ." Then he praised his sport, and he ended, "There's been so many lovely things said

about me, I'm glad I had the opportunity to thank everybody. Thank you."

Ruth made it back at the end of 1947 for the first old-timers' game in history, and then struggled back onto the field in the spring of 1948 for another reunion. He died on August 16, 1948, at the age of 53.

In the house that Ruth built and Gehrig filled, the sepulchral echoes still contain Ruth's belly laughs and Gehrig's poignant speech. The Yankees first two great stars, No. 3 and No. 4, are forever young. In no small way, their mortality enhances the mysteriously enduring Yankee mystique.

Right: Lou Gehrig and Babe Ruth, the first two stars of the team, remain immortal in the folklore of the team.

Bottom: Babe Ruth was honored at the 25th anniversary of the opening of Yankee Stadium in 1947. He died two months later.

Part Two

GEHRIG—DIMAGGIO

(1930s, 40s, 50s)

By *Dave Anderson*

BABE RUTH had not been around the Yankees since his departure, but now, out of baseball as the 1936 season approached, he stopped in St. Petersburg, Florida, to visit the Yankees in spring training. Moving through the clubhouse but forgetful of names, he greeted most of the Yankees with "Hiya, kid . . . hiya, kid," including some who had been teammates. Eventually he stopped at the locker of the 21-year-old rookie outfielder he had never seen before.

"Hiya, Joe," the Babe said.

Until his death in 1999, Joseph Paul DiMaggio marvelled that the Babe had known his name that day. Neither realized that the 21-year-old rookie outfielder's name would endure for 63 years as a living symbol of the Yankees, much longer than the Babe had. And longer than any of the other most famous Yankees had.

The Babe joined the Yankees in 1920 and died in 1948, a span of 28 years. Lou Gehrig took over at first base in 1925 and died in 1941, a span of only 16 years. Mickey Mantle arrived in 1951 and died in 1995, a span of 44 years.

But for more than six decades, Joe DiMaggio, alias the Yankee Clipper, alias Jolting Joe, alias the Jolter, alias Joe D, flourished as only a baseball icon can. As a slugger whose Yankee teams won nine of their 10 World Series and whose record 56-game hitting streak in 1941 still appears unbreakable. As Marilyn Monroe's husband. And

finally as baseball's "Greatest Living Player," the way he was introduced at Old-timers' Day or when he went to the mound at Yankee Stadium to throw out the ceremonial first pitch at a World Series. Through it all, he was shy and serious.

Joe DiMaggio, alias the Yankee Clipper, alias Jolting Joe, alias the Jolter, alias Joe D, flourished as only a baseball icon can for more than six decades.

"When he walked into the clubhouse, the lights flickered," Pete Sheehy, the legendary clubhouse man, once said of Joe DiMaggio.

"I'm not one of those guys," he once told me, "who look to be in the limelight." Instead, the limelight looked for him and inspired songs. His 56-game streak prompted Alan Courtney to write the lyrics and Les Brown's band to record, "Joe, Joe DiMaggio, we want you on our side—we dream of Joey with the light brown bat." Two decades later, in his song "Mrs. Robinson," Paul Simon chirped, "Where have you gone, Joe DiMaggio? A nation turns its lonely eyes to you."

Simon's lyrics confused DiMaggio until they discussed them in a chance meeting at a New York restaurant. DiMaggio, who had taken the lines literally, told him, "I haven't gone anywhere." Simon explained that he thought of DiMaggio as "an American hero, and that genuine heroes were in short supply."

He inspired Ernest Hemingway, when writing *The Old Man and the Sea*, to have Santiago, the Cuban with a skiff in the Gulf Stream, yearn, "I would like to take the great DiMaggio fishing. They say his father was a fisherman. Maybe he was as poor as we are and would understand."

In his pinstriped Yankee uniform, the great DiMaggio, at a lean six feet two inches, and 193 pounds, always looked the part. When he settled into his wide-legged stance in the batter's box, he pumped the bat once, then held it still as he stared at the pitcher. He swung quickly but smoothly, with a sweeping follow-through. Over his 13 seasons from the midst of the Depression in 1936 to the post–World War II boom in 1951, he batted .325 with 361 homers (and only 369 strikeouts, a remarkable ratio). He drove in 1,537 runs.

As a centerfielder when Yankee Stadium's meadows were much more expansive than now, the great DiMaggio glided to flyballs with the grace of a gazelle.

And for more than six decades, the great DiMaggio always dressed the part, usually in a dark suit with a French-cuffed white shirt, a tasteful tie and glossy black shoes. In the winter a navy blue cashmere or camel's hair overcoat would be draped over one arm.

"When he walked into the clubhouse, the lights flickered," Pete Sheehy, the legendary Yankee clubhouse man, once said. "Then he'd turn to me and say, 'Half a cup.'"

DiMaggio meant half a cup of coffee, then he would drink more than a dozen of those half cups. "It stays hot that way," he explained. Decades later, he was seen in television commercials as "Mr. Coffee," shilling for a coffee maker, and as a spokesman for the Bowery Savings Bank. But no matter what he did, it magnified his mystique. He always maintained his privacy and his dignity. During the baseball memorabilia boom, he signed baseballs, bats and photos for the millions of dollars he never made as a player, but whenever a book publisher asked him to do his autobiography, he never sold his memories of Marilyn Monroe, the Hollywood goddess he was married to for 274 days.

"They want me to write about Marilyn," he once told me. "I don't want to do that. I'll never do that."

That's maintaining your privacy (and hers), which DiMaggio did even better than he played baseball. Just as he also maintained his pride the night his 56-game hitting streak was stopped in Cleveland, when Indian third baseman Ken Keltner positioned himself deep behind the bag. Keltner was daring him to bunt for a hit to prolong the streak.

"I hadn't bunted," he said, "during the whole streak."

DiMaggio didn't bunt that night as Keltner turned two sizzling grounders into outs as 67,468 cheered. But he didn't need a sold-out stadium to justify his pride. In the years when the St. Louis Browns were in the American League, he was sitting in the dugout before a Sunday doubleheader at old Sportsman's Park when he was asked how he was always able to perform at such a level of excellence. He gestured toward the half-filled grandstand.

"Maybe some of those people," he said quietly, "never saw me play before."

That's maintaining your ego, which all the great athletes have, but Joe DiMaggio did it with a blend of dignity and style. His teammate Bobby Brown, later the American League president, best described that blend.

"Joe goes through life scared to death people will ask for his autograph," Brown said. "And scared to death they won't."

He has been portrayed as distant and aloof, nasty and vindictive. And maybe he was at times, but I never found him that way. I began covering New York's baseball teams in 1952, the year after his final season, so I never knew him as a player other than having seen him in a few Yankee games. I never talked to him until 1961 when I was writing an article for *Sports Illustrated* on his hitting streak. I had contacted some of his Yankee teammates and had researched the New York newspapers, but now I needed his memories. He was staying at the Lexington Hotel in Manhattan when I phoned to request an interview.

"How long will this take?" he asked.

"Half an hour," I said, hoping for at least twice that. "I've got all my questions ready. I can be there at five-thirty."

"All right," he said. "Half an hour."

When I knocked on the door of his suite at 5:30, there was no answer. I knocked again. No answer. I knocked again. This time, I heard some movement inside the suite. Soon the door opened. As it did, DiMaggio, in a burgundy silk dressing gown and slippers, ushered a tall willowy blonde out the door and ushered me in.

"Half an hour," he reminded me.

An hour and a half later, DiMaggio was still telling me stories about his hitting streak. And whenever I needed to interview him after that, whether for a chapter on him in "The Yankees: The Four Fabulous Eras of Baseball's Most Famous Team" (Random House, 1979) or for various "Sports of The Times" columns, he was always gracious and helpful. In the Yankee Stadium catacombs before an Old-timers' Day, I offered to do an interview on the phone when he returned to Florida if that was more convenient.

"No," he said. "Let's go up to Steinbrenner's office after I throw out the ball."

In his final years, DiMaggio's business dealings and appearance schedule were sheltered by Morris Engelberg, a Hollywood, Florida, attorney. Engelberg even renamed his office building "Yankee Clipper Center." I visited DiMaggio there in 1998 for what turned out to be his last lengthy interview before his illness and death. When we left for lunch at nearby Memorial Regional Hospital with its Joe DiMaggio Children's Wing, we walked toward a white Dodge Caravan with the words "The Yankee Clipper" in navy blue above the rear window. The license plate read "DiMAG 5."

"Is this yours, Morris?" I asked.

"Yes," Engelberg said.

The Yankee Clipper himself turned to me and chuckled. "You don't think it'd be mine, do you?" he asked.

Eight months later, on March 8, 1999, Joe DiMaggio died of lung cancer. His funeral was at SS. Peter and Paul Roman Catholic Church in San Francisco, where he went to grammar school. His father had moved the family across the bay from Martinez, California, where the young Giuseppe, the fourth son and the eighth of nine children, had been born to Giuseppe and Rosalie on November 25, 1914.

Among the mourners outside, an 85-year-old retired maintenance man gestured toward a lot next to the church. "He grew up here and played on this playground," Victor Berardelli said. "He never forgot where he came from."

Joe DiMaggio on the family fishing boat in San Francisco with his brother, Mike. Joe preferred baseball to fishing.

THE SAN FRANCISCO KID

When Joe DiMaggio was growing up in San Francisco, his father Giuseppe's boat had his mother's name, Rosalie D, painted across the stern. Giuseppe, small with a mustache, and Rosalie were from Isola delle Femmine, an islet off Palmero, Sicily, where generations of DiMaggios had fished. Not long after Rosalie's father had immigrated to Collinsville, a town between San Francisco and Sacramento, he wrote her that Giusseppe could make a better living there.

"I'll try it for a year," Giuseppe told his wife.

At the time Rosalie was pregnant with their first child, Nellie, and the next year Giuseppe's wife and daughter joined him in Martinez on San Pablo Bay north of the Oakland-Berkeley area. They would have eight more children: Mamie, Tom, Marie, Michael, Frances, Vincent, Joseph and Dominic, and move to San Francisco, where they lived in a cramped four-room apartment on Taylor Street in the North Beach neighborhood not far from Fisherman's Wharf.

As soon as Joe was old enough, he joined Tom and Michael on their father's boat, but Joe often got seasick. He preferred to play baseball, but at first his father didn't see a responsible future for him in baseball.

His older brother Vince was different. Vince could sing. His parents even considered sending him to Italy for operatic training. Whatever the reason, they didn't complain when he wanted to play baseball. He would hit 125 homers for four National League teams (Boston, Cincinnati, Pittsburgh and Philadelphia) in a 10-year career. But when Vince was a 20-year-old outfielder with the hometown San Francisco Seals, Joe was 17, a

Joe DiMaggio batted .398 with 34 homers and 154 runs batted in when he played in the Pacific Coast League in 1935.

Frank Crosetti, Tony Lazzeri and Joe DiMaggio gave their Italian-American
fans a lot to cheer for at Yankee Stadium.

dropout from Galileo High School who hit .633 that year as a shortstop for the Rossi Olive Oil sandlot team.

Left: The day that Joe DiMaggio arrived at spring training, Lou Gehrig told him, "Nice to have you with us, Joe."

"I didn't work for them; that was just the company that bought our uniforms. But I had a few jobs," Joe once said. "I crated oranges for one day. I picked crabmeat in a cannery for a day. I got $3 for picking shrimp."

Not long after Vince joined the Seals, the other

Joe DiMaggio would later say that the 1936 team was the best of all the Yankee teams he played for. Some of these Yankees were, from left, Bill Dickey, Lou Gehrig, DiMaggio and Tony Lazzeri.

San Francisco team in the Pacific Coast League, the Missions, offered Joe $150 a month. His father agreed, but Joe wanted to talk to Vince, who was at Seals Stadium that day. With no money for a ticket, Joe was peeking through a hole in the fence when a Seal scout, Spike Hennessey, noticed him. Inside, Hennessey introduced Joe to the Seals' owner, Charlie Graham, as a "good-looking prospect" who was Vince's brother.

"You're big for your age," Graham said. "How'd you like to work out with the Seals?"

After that workout, the Seals invited Joe to finish the season. Even though he had no contract and no salary, Joe agreed. That wouldn't happen today but at the time, long before the New York Giants franchise arrived in San Francisco after the 1957 season, the hometown minor-league Seals were the city's most important baseball team. And Vince would be his teammate. His first time up in a PCL game, Joe smashed a triple.

"Sign with us for next year," Graham told him, "and we'll give you $225 a month."

That was big money for an 18-year-old and he earned it, leading the PCL with 169 runs batted in while hitting .340 with 28 homers. More remarkably, he had a 61-game hitting streak that would reduce the pressure of his later 56-game streak with the Yankees. But in the 1934 season,

while getting out of a taxi after having dinner at the home of one of his married sisters, he stumbled and fell. The pain in his left knee was excruciating.

"I didn't realize," he said later, "that the way I

Joe DiMaggio batted .346, slugged 46 homers and drove in 167 runs in 1937.

was sitting in the taxi, my left foot had fallen asleep."

Eventually the diagnosis was torn cartilage. Despite his .341 average, several major-league teams shied away from negotiating with the Seals for him. The offers had soared to $75,000, an awesome price in that era, but now only the Yankees were still interested. Two of their scouts, Joe Devine and Bill Essick, had touted him to Ed Barrow, the Yankees' general manager.

"Don't back off because of the kid's knee," Essick said. "He'll be all right. And you can get him cheap."

When Barrow phoned Graham, the Seals', owner requested $40,000, but Barrow offered half that. They compromised at $25,000 and five players (outfielder Ted Norbert, first baseman Les Powers, third baseman Ed Farrell, pitchers Jim Densmore and Floyd Newkirk) with two provisos: that DiMaggio's knee be checked by Dr. Richard Spencer, a Los Angeles orthopedist, and that he would remain with the Seals in 1935. When Dr. Spencer predicted that DiMaggio would make a full recovery, the Yankees had a deal. And a bargain.

At age 20, DiMaggio burned up the PCL in 1935, batting .398 with 34 homers and driving in 154 runs. He was ready for the Yankees, and they needed him.

Under manager Joe McCarthy, the Yankees had won the pennant and the World Series in 1932, but in each of the previous three seasons, they had finished second. The day that DiMaggio arrived at spring training, Lou Gehrig told him, "Nice to have you with us, Joe." But Red Ruffing, the ace righthander, stared at him.

"So you're the great DiMaggio," Ruffing said.

The rookie's expression didn't change. He

Yankees celebrate in the dressing room after defeating the New York Giants, 4-2, in the fifth and final game of the World Series, October 10, 1937. From left are manager Joe McCarthy, owner Jacob Ruppert, Lou Gehrig and Tony Lazzeri. Joe DiMaggio is in the foreground.

Joe DiMaggio listening to owner Jacob Ruppert. Joe received a $25,000 salary, with Ruppert's blessing, in 1938.

knew that all his PCL headlines didn't mean anything now, that what he did as a Yankee was all that counted. And when the season opened, he wasn't able to play. He had twisted his left foot, then a diathermy lamp had burned it. He missed the first 16 games. Finally, as the leftfielder on May 3 against the Browns at Yankee Stadium, he had a triple and two singles in a 14–5 victory. Six weeks later, after centerfielder Ben Chapman was traded to the Washington Senators for Jake Powell, McCarthy moved DiMaggio to center.

"I wanted him to be comfortable before I put him in center," McCarthy explained. "He needed the room in center to roam, especially in Yankee Stadium, the toughest centerfield in baseball. There's so much ground out there, only the great ones can play it."

The Yankees had a great one who would play it better than anyone else ever has. And in the midst of the Depression, their fans, especially their Italian-American fans, also had an ethnic icon to cheer. In the lineup for the remaining 138 games, DiMaggio batted .323 with 206 hits, including 29 homers. He knocked in 125 runs and scored 132. The Yankees finished first by 19½ games, then won the World Series against the rival New York Giants in six games.

"That team," DiMaggio would say years later, "was the best of all the Yankee teams I played on."

Gehrig batted .354 with 49 homers and 152 RBI, earning the Most Valuable Player Award. Four other eventual Hall of Famers were on that

Babe Ruth, left, shakes hands with Joe DiMaggio, at a banquet in New York on
January 24, 1938. Sportswriter Bill Corum stood between the two.

team—catcher Bill Dickey, second baseman Tony Lazzeri and pitchers Red Ruffing and Lefty Gomez. And in 1937, instead of being afflicted by what is known in baseball as the sophomore jinx, DiMaggio got better, as the great ones usually do. He raised his average to .346, slugged 46 homers and drove in 167 runs.

His teammates also thrived. Gehrig batted .351 with 37 homers and knocked in 159 runs. Dickey hit .332 with 29 homers and 133 runs batted in. Ruffing was 20–7 and Johnny Murphy earned his "Fireman" nickname with 10 saves as well as a 13–4 record. The rookie rightfielder was Tommy Henrich, up from the Newark farm team in the International League.

When the Yankees won the World Series again, in five games against the rival Giants, their young centerfielder believed he deserved a big raise.

Joe DiMaggio relaxing with Charlie Keller, who joined the team
in 1939 and batted .334 with 11 homers.

His salaries had been $8,000 as a rookie, then
$15,000 plus a winning World Series share each
year of about $6,400. In an era nearly forty years
before free agency and before baseball players
had agents to negotiate their contracts, he
stopped by Ed Barrow's office in the weeks
before spring training in 1938 and told the general manager that he wanted $40,000.

"Young man," Barrow said, "do you realize that

Lou Gehrig only makes $43,000 a year after 13
years?"

"In that case, Mr. Barrow," DiMaggio said
respectfully, "Mr. Gehrig is a very underpaid
ballplayer."

Barrow, with Colonel Jake Ruppert's blessing,
offered $25,000 but when spring training began,
DiMaggio stayed in San Francisco, where his
restaurant on Fisherman's Wharf had opened the

previous year. With his restaurant business brisk, he bluffed that he could not afford to leave, but his absence from spring training annoyed his teammates. Most of them considered $25,000 a generous salary for a third-year player, even one with DiMaggio's production. When the Yankees arrived in New York to open the season, Joe Gould, a boxing manager who knew DiMaggio, phoned him.

"You have a chance this year to break a lot of records and then get the money you want," Gould said. "But you can't break any records in San Francisco."

The next day DiMaggio agreed to the $25,000 offer. When he put on his Yankee uniform, he heard boos from the Depression-stricken fans who resented his "greedy" demands. Those same fans soon were cheering him. As the Yankees breezed to their third consecutive pennant, he hit .324, drove in 140 runs and slugged 32 homers. Joe Gordon, a rookie second baseman up from Newark, hit 25 homers. Ruffing was 21–7, Gomez 18–12, right-hander Monte Pearson 16–7, including a 13–0 no-hitter aganst the Indians. Then the Yankees swept the Cubs in the World Series, their third straight.

In 1939 the Yankees faced two shocks of mortality. Jake Ruppert died on January 13, the club passing into the control of the colonel's estate. Six months later, Gehrig, the Iron Horse, was discovered to be fatally ill. His consecutive-game streak ended on May 2 in Detroit, at 2,130 games. He would die two years later.

"It was sad to see," DiMaggio said later of Gehrig's illness, amyotrophic lateral sclerosis, that is now named for him. "At spring training in 1939 he suddenly couldn't hit anymore. He'd swing and miss, or he'd hit a hump line drive. He had no power. One time he went to sit down in the dugout and missed the bench."

When Gehrig took himself out of the lineup, the new first baseman was Ellsworth (Babe) Dahlgren, who drove in 89 runs. The new left-fielder was Charlie Keller, who batted .334 with 11 homers. DiMaggio, meanwhile, earned his first Most Valuable Player Award with his first batting title and the highest average of his career, .381, along with 30 homers and 126 runs batted in. Gordon had 28 homers and 111 RBI; Dickey, 24 and 105; Selkirk, 21 and 101. Third baseman Red Rolfe's 139 runs scored led the league. Ruffing was 21–7, rookie right-hander Atley Donald 13–3 after opening with 12 consecutive victories. Pearson was 12–5, Gomez 12–8, Bump Hadley 12–6, Steve Sundra 11–1, Oral Hildebrand 10–4—seven pitchers with at least 10 victories. With a 4–0 sweep of the Cincinnati Reds, the Yankees were the first to win four straight World Series, the last two in eight consecutive games.

But in 1940 the Yankees struggled. Although they won 16 of 19 to move into first place after the opener of a September 11 doubleheader in Cleveland, they drifted to an 88–66 finish, third behind the Tigers and the Indians.

With a .352 average, DiMaggio won his second and last batting title while hitting 31 homers and driving in 133 runs. Gordon had 30 homers with 103 runs batted in, Keller 21 homers with 93 RBI and Henrich hit .307, but Dickey skidded to .247 with only 9 homers. Ruffing was 15–12 while Gomez's sore arm dropped him to 3–3. The new Yankee starter was Ernest (Tiny) Bonham, who led the league with a 1.90 ERA and produced a 9–3 record after his promotion from Kansas City of the American Association.

But whatever happened in 1940 was merely a prelude to 1941, the season that will always belong to Joe DiMaggio.

Lefty Gomez working out with his roommate Joe DiMaggio.

THE STREAK

In the summer of 1941, harsh reality intruded on the baseball season. Although nobody in America realized it, Japanese admirals were plotting their Pearl Harbor attack. President Franklin Delano Roosevelt described a "national emergency" and warned of Hitler's plan to "extend his Nazi domination to the Western Hemisphere." In the coastal cities, a new sound was heard: the whining wail of air-raid sirens signaling test blackouts. Even so, there was always time to sing a silly tune, "Hut Sut Rawlson on the Rillerah." And there was always time to check whether Joe DiMaggio got his hit.

But in the middle of May, the two-time batting champion was down to .306 while the Yankees had lost four straight and seven of their last nine. They were in fourth place, 5½ games behind the league-leading Indians.

At the Stadium on the afternoon of May 15, the Yankees lost again, 13–1, but in the first inning DiMaggio got a single off Edgar Smith, the stocky White Sox left-hander. His record 56-game hitting streak had begun, but the Yankees' slump was the story. Two weeks later, in the Memorial Day doubleheader in Boston, his fielding was the story. He made four errors—a dropped flyball in the opener, a fumbled grounder and two wild throws in the second game. Four errors by arguably the smoothest centerfielder ever. Only

his roommate, Lefty Gomez, knew that he was bothered by a swollen neck.

"I get it every year," DiMaggio said. "It'll go away."

On the evening of June 2, as the Yankees arrived at the Book-Cadillac in Detroit, the hotel manager informed Joe McCarthy that Lou Gehrig had died. McCarthy and Dickey, who had been Gehrig's roommate, returned to New York for the June 4 funeral. When McCarthy rejoined the Yankees in St. Louis for a weekend series with the Browns, he discussed DiMaggio's role. "The boys," the manager said, "are just waiting for Joe to show 'em how to do it."

That day DiMaggio had three hits. In a double-header the next day, he crashed three homers and a double. Suddenly the Yankees had an eight-game winning streak and DiMaggio had a 24-game hitting streak. The club record was 29 games, shared by shortstop Roger Peckinpaugh and centerfielder Earle Combs.

"That's when I became conscious of the streak, when the writers started talking about the records I could break," DiMaggio recalled. "But at that stage, I didn't think too much about it."

The following week, on June 17, he broke the Yankee record with a bad-hop single off the shoulder of White Sox shortstop Luke Appling—one of the rare times luck helped. But by now DiMaggio was a national celebrity. When he and his New York ticket-broker pal, George Solitaire, went to the first Joe Louis–Billy Conn heavy-weight title fight at the Polo Grounds, he needed a police escort to keep the fans away.

"There were so many people asking for his

Mayor Fiorello La Guardia of New York presents Joe DiMaggio with a gold watch and a citation award as the most valuable baseball player in the American League during the 1939 season. The presentation was made at the Yankee–Cleveland Indians game on August 23, 1940, at Yankee Stadium.

autograph," Solitaire once said, "he had almost as many cops around him as the fighters did on their way into the ring."

Other records loomed. In 1922 George Sisler, the Browns' first baseman, hit in 41 straight games for the American League record. That same year Rogers Hornsby had a 33-game streak for the modern National League record, but in 1897 Wee Willie Keeler hit in 44 games for the Baltimore Orioles, then an NL team—the major-league record that DiMaggio was most aware of. But all the commotion didn't seem to faze him, perhaps because he had already been through a 61-game streak with the San Francisco Seals.

"I never saw a guy so calm," Gomez said. "I wound up with the upset stomachs."

Against the Tigers on July 20 at the Stadium, DiMaggio had four hits, matching Hornsby's streak and raising his average to .354. In the 37th game, his eighth-inning single preserved the streak against Bob Muncrief, the Browns' rookie right-hander.

"It wouldn't have been fair to walk him—to him or to me," Muncrief said. "Hell, he's the greatest player I ever saw."

Two days later, June 26, after the Yankees had finally ascended into first place, they were leading the Browns, 3–1, going into the bottom of the eighth inning. In three at-bats against Eldon Auker, a submarine-ball right-hander, DiMaggio was hitless. Unless the Yankees had a baserunner in the eighth, he would not get up again. First baseman Johnny Sturm popped up, but when Rolfe walked, Henrich looked into the dugout from the on-deck circle.

"If I hit into a double play, Joe won't get up," he reminded McCarthy. "Is it all right if I bunt?"

McCarthy nodded. Henrich bunted, moving Rolfe to second. On the first pitch, DiMaggio drilled a double to left. Two days later, June 28,

right-hander Johnny Babich was the Philadelphia Athletics pitcher. The previous season he had beaten the Yankees five times and now he had bragged that he would stop the streak.

"Even if it meant walking me every time up," DiMaggio often said.

His first at-bat, DiMaggio walked. His next time up, Babich threw three wide fastballs. Stepping out of the batter's box and staring at third-base coach Art Fletcher, DiMaggio hoped he would be allowed to swing at the 3–0 pitch. Fletcher, relaying a signal from McCarthy, flashed the "hit" sign.

"The next pitch was outside, too," DiMaggio said, "but I lined it between's Babich's legs. After I took my turn at first, I looked over at him. His face was white as a sheet."

The next day, at Griffith Stadium in Washington, DiMaggio tied Sisler at 41 games with a double off knuckleballer Dutch Leonard in the opener of a doubleheader. Between games, a young fan hopped onto the field near the Yankee dugout, grabbed DiMaggio's favorite bat and disappeared into the stands. In the seventh inning of the second game, DiMaggio used Henrich's bat, a DiMaggio model, and singled to left. With a hit in his 42nd straight game, he set the AL record, but he bemoaned the theft of his favorite bat.

"Most of my models are 36 inches long and weigh 36 ounces," he said, "but I had sandpapered the handle of this one to take off one-half to three-quarters of an ounce. It was just right. I wish that guy would return it. I need it more than he does."

Although the thief was never identified, a young man in Newark, New Jersey, made the mistake of bragging about having stolen the bat. When he was confronted by men described by DiMaggio only as "good friends of mine," he surrendered the bat, which was returned to Yankee Stadium in time for DiMaggio to challenge

All the commotion about his hitting streak in 1941 did not faze Joe DiMaggio because he had been through a 61-game streak with the San Francisco Seals, his minor-league team.

Keeler's 44-game record in a July 1 doubleheader with the Red Sox. In time, too, for an official scorer's dilemma. In the opener, third baseman Jim Tabor fielded DiMaggio's tricky grounder but his hurried throw flew past first base. The official scorer, Dan Daniel of *The New York World-Telegram*, raised his right arm. Hit.

"That was one of the few times I got a break from the scorer on a questionable play," DiMaggio recalled. "Instead of giving me the benefit of the doubt—not that I was asking for it— they usually made sure it was a clean hit."

Although the second game was rained out after five innings, his single off right-hander Jack Wilson in the first inning counted. He had tied Keeler's record. The next day, he broke it. Against right-hander Heber (Dick) Newsome, a 19-game winner that season, he hit his 18th homer into the lower left field stands. As he crossed home plate, he tipped his cap to the ovation from 52,832 at the Stadium and turned toward the Yankee dugout, then behind third base, where Gomez and his teammates were waiting.

"You not only broke Keeler's record; you even

Joe DiMaggio and Ted Williams of the Red Sox chatting before a doubleheader at Yankee Stadium on July 1, 1941.

Joe DiMaggio celebrates with teammates on July 2, 1941, after breaking Wee Willie Keeler's record of hitting in 44 consecutive games.

used his formula," Gomez told him. "You hit 'em where they ain't."

At his locker later, DiMaggio sipped his half a cup of coffee, lit a cigarette and reflected on the record.

"I don't know how far I can go," he said, "but I'm not going to worry about it now. I'm glad I've got the record; it got to be quite a strain the last ten days. I was swinging at some bad pitches so I wouldn't be walked, but now I can go back to swinging at good pitches."

When he left the Stadium late that afternoon, he needed a police escort to get to Gomez's waiting car for the ride to his West Side apartment.

"That apartment," Gomez said years later. "Remember how in those days every time a guy hit a home run, they gave him a case of Wheaties cereal? I once opened the door to an extra closet

Joe DiMaggio scores on July 16, 1941, against the Cleveland Indians. He had
three hits to extend his hitting streak to 56 games.

in Joe's apartment, and there were cases of Wheaties up to the ceiling."

By the time DiMaggio arrived in Detroit for the All-Star Game, the streak was at 48 games. His double there didn't count as part of the streak, but his force-out drove in the fourth run just before Ted Williams walloped a three-run homer for a 7–5 victory.

When the Yankees opened a three-game series in St. Louis on July 10, three-column newspaper ads announced: THE SENSATIONAL JOE DIMAGGIO WILL ATTEMPT TO HIT SAFELY IN HIS 49TH CONSECUTIVE GAME TONIGHT!

He did just that, with a single off Johnny Niggeling, a knuckleballing right-hander. The next day, he had four hits, including a homer, for the fourth time in the streak. The Yankees moved on to Chicago and then to Cleveland, where the Indians split their home schedule between little old League Park and, for their more attractive dates, huge Municipal Stadium. On a quiet Wednesday afternoon in League Park, he had three hits to extend the streak to 56 games.

Late the next afternoon, as DiMaggio and Gomez hunched into a taxi for the short ride from the Hotel Cleveland to Municipal Stadium, the driver recognized DiMaggio and blurted, "I got a feeling if you don't get a hit the first time up, they're going to stop you tonight." DiMaggio didn't say anything but Gomez snapped, "What the hell is this? What are you trying to do, jinx him?"

The Indians' pitcher was Al Smith, a crafty lefthander who would post a 12–13 record that season. But many of the 67,468 fans were hoping that DiMaggio would get a hit that night so that the streak would still be on the line the next afternoon against Bob Feller, who was roaring to a 25–13 record with 260 strikeouts. In the first inning, it appeared that DiMaggio had his hit—a sharp grounder down the third-base line that seemed beyond the reach of Ken Keltner, positioned deep on the infield dirt. But the Indians' third baseman lunged to his right, snatched the ball backhanded and, from foul ground, threw DiMaggio out.

In the Yankee dugout, Gomez grumbled, "That cab driver, that lousy cab driver."

His next time up, DiMaggio walked. In the seventh he drilled another hot grounder at Keltner, who threw him out again. In the eighth, the Yankees knocked out Smith and took a 4–3 lead. With DiMaggio up next, Indian manager Roger Peckinpaugh, the onetime Yankee shortstop who had shared the Yankee record for hitting in 29 consecutive games, waved to the bullpen for Jim Bagby Jr., a young right-hander who would be 9–15 that season.

On a 2–1 count, DiMaggio hit another sharp grounder that took a high hop, but shortstop Lou Boudreau grabbed it and started a double play.

As DiMaggio rounded first base, he knew the streak had probably ended, but he just picked up his glove (in those years, fielders left their gloves on the outfield grass between innings) and trotted toward center field. He didn't kick the dirt. He didn't shake his head.

The streak was over, but he was still Joe DiMaggio. Still serene. Still controlled.

As he reached into his locker for a cigarette after that game, he was heard to say softly, "Well, that's over." When the newspapermen soon surrounded him, he said, "I can't say that I'm glad it's over. I wanted it to go on as long as it could." So did his teammates. During those 56 games, he had batted .408 with 91 hits, including 16 doubles, 4 triples and 15 homers; he had scored 56 runs and driven in 55 runs. He had 160 total bases. Even more remarkably, he had struck out only seven times. And the Yankees had a 41–13 record (two games ended in a no-decision) for a stunning .759 percentage that took command of the pennant race.

The end of the streak didn't deflate DiMaggio. The next day, against Bob Feller, he started another one that lasted 16 games, of which the Yankees won 14; it ended August 3, when Johnny Niggeling of the Browns stopped him at the stadium in the opener of a doubleheader—the only doubleheader the Yankees lost all season.

Over those two streaks, DiMaggio batted safely in 72 of 73 games. From May 2 until Niggeling stopped him, he had been on base in 83 consecutive games and the Yankees were on their way to finishing 17 games ahead of the second-place Red Sox—the main reason why DiMaggio received the Most Valuable Player Award over Ted Williams, who batted .406, the last major leaguer to hit .400 or above. In the Baseball Writers' Association of America voting, DiMaggio had 291 points, Williams 254.

DiMaggio batted .357, third in the AL behind Williams and Senators shortstop Cecil Travis, who hit .359, but the Jolter led the league with 125 runs batted in and 348 total bases. He had 43 doubles, 11 triples and 30 homers, with only 13 strikeouts.

Of the other Yankees, Keller flourished with 33 homers and 122 runs batted in, Henrich had 31

Manager Joe McCarthy and his team congratulate Joe DiMaggio after
his 56-game hitting streak ended in Cleveland on July 17, 1941.

homers and 85 RBI, Gordon 24 homers and 87 RBI and their tiny rookie shortstop, Phil Rizzuto, hit .307. Ruffing was 15–6, Gomez 15–5, Marius Russo 14–10, Murphy 8–3 with a 1.98 earned-run average and 15 saves. But less than a week before the Yankees would clinch the pennant and more than a month before the league's MVP votes were cast, DiMaggio's teammates honored him in their own way. When the Yankees checked into

the Hotel Shoreham in Washington on August 29, they had the night off. DiMaggio and Gomez planned to have dinner in the hotel but Gomez took a long shower.

"C'mon, Lefty, let's go," DiMaggio said. "All the steaks will be gone."

With a wisecrack, Gomez still took his time. Then on the way to the elevator, he remembered that he had to stop by George Selkirk's room.

A third strike gets past Dodger catcher Mickey Owen as Tommy Henrich runs to first in Game 4 of the 1941 World Series. The Yankees took advantage of the miscue and would go on to win the World Series.

"I'll get a table and order," DiMaggio grumbled. "No, stay with me," Gomez said. "Stay with me."

As the door to room 609D swung open, DiMaggio saw nearly forty men with raised champagne glasses. After cheers and songs, Gomez presented his roommate with a gift-wrapped package. Inside was a sterling silver cigar humidor. Atop the cover was a silver statuette of the Yankee centerfielder in his classic swing. On one side was "56" for the number of games in the streak; on the other was "91" for the number of his hits in the streak.

"Presented to Joe DiMaggio," the inscription read, "by his fellow players on the New York Yankees to express their admiration for his consecutive-game hitting record, 1941." Below were the engraved autographs of all his teammates.

About two weeks earlier, Bill Dickey had sug-

Joe DiMaggio and his first wife, Dorothy Arnold, enjoy
Joe Jr.'s first Christmas in 1941.

gested to Johnny Murphy, George Selkirk and Tommy Henrich that the team should do "something special" to honor the streak. Now, in room 609D, Murphy offered a toast, saying, "Joe, we just wanted you to know how proud we are to be playing on a ball club with you and that we think your hitting streak won the pennant for us." Seeing DiMaggio staring at the humidor, Murphy smiled.

"We got it at Tiffany's," he said.

Looking around at his teammates, DiMaggio said, "This is swell, but I don't deserve it." But he cherished that humidor and that party more than any of the dozens of other awards, trophies or plaques that he received in his lifetime.

"It was just a little party in a hotel room," he once said, "but it was the biggest party I'll ever go to."

For all the excitement of DiMaggio's streak,

when the 1941 World Series approached, the Yankees were playing second fiddle to the Brooklyn Dodgers, who had won their first National League pennant since 1920. Managed by Leo Durocher, once a Yankee shortstop, the team known affectionately in some New York newspapers as "Dem Bums" featured Dolph Camilli at first base, Pete Reiser in centerfield, Harold (Pee Wee) Reese at shortstop and Whitlow Wyatt on the mound. The Yankees took the opener at the Stadium 3–2 behind Ruffing but Wyatt won the second game, also 3–2—the Yankees' first Series defeat after 10 consecutive victories since 1937.

In Ebbets Field, the Yankees got two breaks. In the seventh inning of the scoreless third game, left-handed pitcher Marius Russo's line drive smashed off Freddie Fitzsimmon's left leg. The ball richocheted to Reese for the third out, but a hobbling Fitzsimmons had to be helped into the dugout. In the eighth, singles by Rolfe, Henrich, DiMaggio and Keller off Hugh Casey generated a 2–1 victory. In the ninth the next day Casey again was pitching, this time with a 4–3 lead, two out and nobody on when he appeared to have Henrich struck out on a lunging swing. But the ball skidded past catcher Mickey Owen for an error as Henrich hurried to first.

With new life, the Yankees pounced. DiMaggio singled sharply to left. Keller, on an 0–2 pitch, doubled off the right-field wall, scoring both Henrich and DiMaggio for a 5–4 lead. Dickey walked. Gordon doubled to left for the 7–4 final score. Stunned and shaken, the Dodgers went out meekly for Murphy in the ninth.

The next day Tiny Bonham wrapped up the Yankees' fifth World Series championship in six years with a 3–1 four-hitter that is remembered

for the *Brooklyn Eagle* headline that would develop into the Dodgers' motto—WAIT 'TIL NEXT YEAR—and for a rare confrontation in which DiMaggio exchanged angry words with an opposing player. In the fifth Henrich hit a homer off Wyatt for a 3–1 lead. Up next, DiMaggio had to pull away from Wyatt's two knockdown pitches before hitting a long flyball that Reiser caught near the center-field wall. As he trotted across the infield grass to the Yankee dugout behind third base, DiMaggio yelled at Wyatt, who yelled back.

Joe DiMaggio stirring a pot of stew as part of his KP duties at the Army reception center at Monterey, California, in February 1943.

Nearly a decade later, Wyatt told Dodger broadcaster Red Barber that Mickey Owen had ordered the two knockdown pitches.

"Mickey told me later," Wyatt explained, "that he heard Joe had said before the game that Mickey had it coming to him for dropping that strike the day before because Mickey had gone out of his way to slide into Rizzuto earlier in that game."

When Barber told DiMaggio of Wyatt's version, he acknowledged his annoyance with Owen.

"I still say," DiMaggio said at the time, "that was a lousy play, that slide into Rizzuto."

Two months later, the Japanese bombed Pearl Harbor. The nation was in World War II on two fronts, Europe and the Pacific, but President Roosevelt asked the major leagues to keep playing in 1942 to bolster the nation's morale, especially servicemen and war-plant workers. Not yet in the military, DiMaggio asked for a raise over the $37,500 he had earned with his 56-game hitting streak. He not only was refused; he was asked to take a $5,000 cut by Ed Barrow, the crusty general manager.

"Soldiers are making $21 a month," Barrow growled to the newspapermen, "but DiMaggio wants a big raise."

Barrow, while quietly telling DiMaggio not to talk to reporters, dispatched the Yankees' traveling secretary, Mark Roth, to the centerfielder's West Side apartment with a contract calling for the same $37,500 salary. DiMaggio eventually got $43,750, but he never forgot that bitter dispute.

"What letters I got after Barrow mentioned the soldiers," he said years later. "Baseball owners ruled with an iron hand then. Now, with the free-agent situation, the shoe is on the other foot. And deservedly so."

DiMaggio reacted with an off year, for him— .305 with 21 homers and 114 runs batted in—as the Yankees finished first by nine games. But for the only time on DiMaggio's 10 pennant-winners, they lost the World Series. After winning the opener from the St. Louis Cardinals, they lost the next four games. And soon DiMaggio was one of those soldiers. Depleted in 1943 by the absence of DiMaggio (Army), Rizzuto (Navy) and Henrich (Coast Guard), the Yankees won the pennant by 13½ games and the World Series rematch with the Cardinals in five games. In 1944 the Yankees dropped to third place, in 1945 to fourth after the Ruppert heirs sold the club to a unlikely triumvirate: playboy millionaire Dan Topping, construction tycoon Del Webb and loud Larry McPhail, once the Dodgers' and Reds' general manager.

But without DiMaggio, the Yankees didn't resemble the Yankees until he returned in 1946.

Joe DiMaggio and his brother Dominic are served a plate of
ravioli by their mother, Rosalie, in 1947.

THE YEARS AFTER THE WAR

Baseball's post–World War II boom began with the 1946 season. Discharged servicemen were home, including the big-league players who had been in the military. Jobs were plentiful. Just about everybody had the money for a good time. And to many people, baseball represented the best possible time, especially with most teams inserting a few night games into their schedule.

College football, boxing and thoroughbred racing each had their appeal, but baseball was America's game. Minor-league teams were everywhere.

Other sports would need time to grow. The National Football League was a decade away from capturing the public's attention. The National Basketball Association was an infant. The National Hockey League was a six-team curiosity—two teams in the Northeast, two in the Midwest, two in Canada.

Baseball, in contrast, had its best players on display again. But some were rusty. Joe DiMaggio didn't even have the highest 1946 batting average in his family—his little brother Dominic did, batting .316 as the bespectacled centerfielder for the pennant-winning Red Sox.

After having missed three seasons, Joe DiMaggio hit .290 with 25 homers and 95 runs batted in as the Yankees stumbled to third place with an 87–67 record. Even though Keller, Gordon, Henrich and Rizzuto had returned, the Yankees had no stability. Uncomfortable with the new Topping-Webb-MacPhail ownership, Joe McCarthy resigned as manager on May 24; Bill Dickey was named his successor. When Dickey resigned on September 12, Johnny Neun completed the confusing season.

But as the Cardinals defeated the Red Sox in the World Series in seven games, DiMaggio's opinion would provide the workhorse of the Yankees' pitching staff for nearly a decade.

Even though Gordon hit only .210 with 11 homers in 1946, the Indians wanted him to be their second baseman alongside Lou Boudreau, their shortstop and young manager. Bill Veeck, the Indians' flamboyant owner, offered the Yankees one of two pitchers—slender 29-year-old right-hander Charles (Red) Embree, 8–12 with a 3.47 earned-run average, or sturdy 31-year-old right-hander Allie Reynolds, 11–15 with a 3.89 ERA. Seeking DiMaggio's advice, Topping asked him which pitcher the Yankees should take.

"Reynolds," DiMaggio replied.

When the Yankees rebounded to win the 1947 pennant, Reynolds was their best pitcher with a 19–8 record, but other reasons existed. Bucky Harris, hired by MacPhail as the new manager, calmed the clubhouse. DiMaggio earned his third

Most Valuable Player Award with a .315 average, 20 homers and 97 runs batted in. George McQuinn, acquired from the Browns, hit .304 and drove in 80 runs as the Yankees' best first baseman since Gehrig. Lawrence Peter Berra, a rookie catcher and sometimes outfielder known as Yogi, hit .280 with 11 homers in only 83 games and displayed a gift for creative language.

"Dickey," he said of the Yankee coach who was tutoring him as a catcher, "is learning me his experience."

But as the Yankees roared to a 97–57 record, their new name was Joe Page, a left-handed relief pitcher with a flaming fastball and a roustabout reputation. As DiMaggio's roommate, Page had been scolded for returning to their hotel room in the wee hours after having pitched poorly in a May 10 game at Fenway Park.

"What the hell are you doing?" DiMaggio barked. "The way you live, you're letting the team down and you're letting yourself down."

The next day DiMaggio requested a single room on road trips, paying the difference between the single and double rates. Two weeks later, on May 26, Page was within one pitch of being banished to the minors. At a Stadium night game before 74,747, the Yankees' single-game attendance record prior to the 1976 remodeling, the Red Sox were leading, 3–1, with nobody out and the bases loaded in the third inning when Page went to 3–0 on first baseman Rudy York. Another ball, Bucky Harris acknowledged later, and Page would have been demoted to the Newark farm team.

The next pitch was a strike. So was the following pitch, then York struck out. Page also went to 3–0 on second baseman Bobby Doerr, who also struck out. When shortstop Eddie Pellegrini flied out, Page had renewed Harris's faith in him.

Joe DiMaggio suggested that the team take Allie Reynolds in a 1947 trade with the Cleveland Indians. DiMaggio's opinion provided the team with the workhorse of the staff for nearly a decade.

The Yankees went on to win that game, 9–3, and Page went on to a 14–8 record with a 2.48 ERA and 17 saves. In the decisive seventh game of the World Series against the Dodgers, he was credited with the victory in relief after allowing only one hit over five innings. He also saved two other triumphs in a Series best remembered for two other moments—Cookie Lavagetto's two-run ninth-inning pinch double that spoiled righthander

Floyd (Bill) Bevens's no-hitter for a 3–2 Dodger victory at Ebbets Field in the fourth game and Al Gionfriddo's catch of DiMaggio's drive near the left-field bullpen at the Stadium in the sixth game.

In those years, a sign reading 415 denoted the distance to the left-field bullpen, in what was known as "Death Valley" to flyballs that would have been home runs in any other ballpark of that era. With the Dodgers leading, 8–5, the

Yankees had two on when DiMaggio crashed a long flyball off left-hander Joe Hatten toward the bullpen. Gionfriddo, inserted that inning for defense, hurried "back, back, back," as Red Barber said, and stabbed at the ball with his glove. DiMaggio, nearly at second base by then, kicked the bag in disgust—one of the few times in his career that he displayed any emotion.

During the Series celebration, MacPhail announced he was selling his one-third interest in the Yankees to Topping and Webb for $2 million. Quite a return on his investment, which had consisted entirely of his baseball know-how.

With a new general manager, George Weiss, promoted from having been in charge of the Yankee farm system, the Yankees finished third in 1948 as the Indians won the pennant in a one-game playoff with the Red Sox. DiMaggio, despite a painful heel ailment, hit .320, crashed 39 homers and led the league with 155 runs batted in. Berra hit .305 with 14 homers and drove in 98 runs. Of the pitchers, right-hander Vic Raschi was 19–8; Eddie Lopat, a soft-stuff left-hander obtained from the White Sox, was 17–11; and Reynolds was 16–7; but Page skidded to 7–8 with a 4.26 earned-run average.

After firing Harris at the end of the season, Weiss hired a longtime pal, Charles Dillon (Casey) Stengel, who would emerge as arguably the Yankees' most famous manager. But the morning after Stengel's appointment was announced, he was described by John Drebinger of *The New York Times* as a "onetime hard-hitting outfielder, manager of both major and minor league clubs, sage, wit, raconteur . . . glib with the wisecrack."

Nobody touted Stengel's acumen as a manager.

Joe Page is surrounded by his teammates at the end of the game as they celebrate their Game 7 victory against the Dodgers in the 1947 World Series.

In nine seasons with the Dodgers and the Braves, his teams had finished as high as fifth only twice. In his 12 seasons in the minors with Worcester, Toledo, Milwaukee, Kansas City and Oakland, his teams had won only two pennants—20 years apart. And when he was introduced as the Yankee manager, he accidentally justified his wit.

"I want first of all," he opened, "to thank Mr. Bob Topping for this opportunity."

Dan Topping was the Yankee co-owner, not his brother Bob, but Dan laughed along with everybody else. DiMaggio laughed, too. He had been asked to attend the news conference in order to suggest his approval. He and Stengel had lunch together that day at Toots Shor's restaurant on West 51st Street. "You're the old standby," the new manager told him. "I'm going to be asking for your help."

"Anything you need from me," the Yankee Clipper replied, "I'll be very happy to give it."

DiMaggio soon was happier than ever with his salary—$100,000 for the 1949 season. He had bone-spur surgery on his right heel in November, but as spring training approached, his heel was bothering him again. He limped through the exhibition games until the pain convinced him to undergo several x-ray treatments and salt injections. For two months he remained mostly in his Mayflower Hotel suite, his heel literally hot. But one morning in June the pain and the heat were gone. Still on the inactive list, he spent several afternoons at Yankee Stadium, taking batting practice and shagging flyballs. His heel was sore, but he had no pain. He had missed the first 65 games, but when the Yankees opened a three-game series in Fenway Park on June 28, he walked into Stengel's office.

"I'm ready," he told the manager, "if you want me."

His first time up against left-hander Maurice (Mickey) McDermott, he slapped a single to left. In the third, he walloped a two-run homer into the screen atop the left-field wall. The next night, he hit two homers. The following afternoon, with a small plane towing a sign reading THE GREAT DIMAGGIO above Fenway Park, he hit another homer. Over the three games, he had four homers, drove in nine runs and scored five as the first-place Yankees opened a 5½-game lead to 8½ over the Red Sox. In the process, his stature had a new dimension.

During the 56–game hitting streak, DiMaggio was primarily an attraction. But in this dazzling comeback from the heel ailment, he had completed a remarkable return from adversity.

In mid-September he would be benched by adversity again. With the Yankees holding a 2½–game lead over the Red Sox, viral pneumonia weakened him. In 10 days he lost 18 pounds, and the Yankees lost their lead. Entering the final two games of the season at the Stadium, the Red Sox had a one-game lead. One victory would clinch the pennant, but by then a weakened DiMaggio was back in the lineup. At what was advertised as "Joe DiMaggio Day" on Saturday, he received an automobile for himself, another for his mother, Rosalie, a yacht and a television set, among other gifts.

When the Yankees won, 5–4, on Joe Page's relief pitching and left-fielder Johnny Lindell's tie-breaking homer, the pennant would be decided in Sunday's game. And the Yankees, behind right-hander Vic Raschi, won that game, 5–3, and the pennant.

In only 76 games, DiMaggio hit 14 homers and knocked in 67 runs. He batted .346, but with only 272 at-bats, he was ineligible for the batting title that George Kell, the Tigers' third baseman, won with a .343 average. In the World Series, the Yankees took the opener, 1–0, on Henrich's walk-

Joe DiMaggio, center, waving a cap, received two automobiles and a yacht
on his special day in 1949. He gave one car to his mother.

off homer against Don Newcombe, the Dodgers' rookie right-hander, and won in five games.

In Casey Stengel's first year, the Yankees had transformed him from clown to genius—at age 60. It would be the first of a record five consecutive World Series championships for the Yankees, yet Stengel emerged as famous for his syntax as for his success.

With DiMaggio healthy again in 1950, batting .301 with 32 homers and 122 RBI, the Yankees posted a 98–56 record, three games ahead of the Tigers. Rizzuto, having his finest season with a .324 average, earned the Most Valuable Player Award. Raschi was 21–8, Lopat 18–8, Reynolds 16–12, left-hander Tommy Byrne 15–9. But the new name among the pitchers was Edward (Whitey) Ford, from Astoria, Queens, a 21-year-old left-hander who was 9–1 after his promotion from the Kansas City farm team in midseason. Ford also completed the four-game sweep of the Phillies in the World Series. But for all the team's success, DiMaggio was seething at Stengel.

The lineup one day had Johnny Mize batting cleanup, with DiMaggio dropped to fifth. Another time Stengel, without asking, decided to rest him; in silent protest, DiMaggio sat in the bullpen. He also played first base one day, after Dan Topping asked him if he would.

The next year, 1951, would be DiMaggio's last season. With a 98–56 record, the Yankees won another pennant, but he slumped to .263 with only 12 homers and 71 runs batted in. The pitching, even with Ford in the Army, was solid. Lopat was 21–9, Raschi 21–10, Reynolds 17–8 with no-hitters against the Indians at Cleveland on July 12 and the Red Sox at the Stadium on September 28—Berra dropped Ted Williams's pop foul for what would have been the final out, but on the next pitch Williams lifted another pop foul that Yogi caught.

In the World Series against the Giants, who had won the NL pennant playoff on Bobby Thomson's three-run homer off Dodger right-hander Ralph Branca, the Yankees won in six games. DiMaggio contributed a homer off Sal Maglie, the Giants' ace, in the fourth game and a double off Larry Jansen, the Giants' other 20-game winner, in the finale in what would be his last at-bat.

Shortly after the Series ended, DiMaggio told Topping and Webb, "I can't play anymore." His career was over. The co-owners told him to take some time to think about it; they also assured his $100,000 salary. Several weeks later, *Life* magazine published what had been the Dodger scout Andy High's report on the Yankees, notably DiMaggio's limitations as both a hitter and a centerfielder:

"Fielding—he can't stop quickly and throw hard. You can take the extra base on him if he is in motion away from the line of throw. He won't throw on questionable plays and I would challenge him even though he threw a man or so out.

"Speed—he can't run and he won't bunt.

"Hitting vs. right-handed pitcher—his reflexes are very slow and he can't pull a good fastball at all. The fastball is better thrown high but that is not too important as long as it is fast. Throw him nothing but good fastballs and fast curveballs. Don't slow up on him.

"Hitting vs. left-handed pitcher—will pull left-hand pitcher a little more than right-hand pitcher. Pitch him the same. Don't slow up on him. He will go for a bad pitch once in a while with two strikes."

In Casey Stengel's first year as the team's manager in 1949, the Yankees transformed him from clown to genius. He won his first of seven World Championships.

In 1951 Joe DiMaggio slumped to .263 with only
12 homers and 71 runs batted in.

The embarrassing scouting report was the straw that broke Joe DiMaggio's pride. On December 12, in the Yankee offices that were then in the Squibb Tower at 745 Fifth Avenue on the corner of East 57th Street, the newspapermen were handed a statement announcing DiMaggio's retirement. He was there along with Topping, Webb and Stengel.

"I'm not Joe DiMaggio anymore," he said.

Joe DiMaggio sits outside the Yankee office on December 12, 1951,
after announcing his retirement as a player. "I'm not Joe DiMaggio anymore,"
he said. On the wall behind Joe was a mural of himself.

Left: Joe DiMaggio hitting his last homer off Giants Sal Maglie at the
Polo Grounds in Game 4 of the 1951 World Series.

Newlyweds Joe DiMaggio and Marilyn Monroe arrive at San Francisco's International Airport, January 29, 1954, prior to their departure for Tokyo for an extension of their honeymoon. They were married in San Francisco on January 14.

MARILYN AND THE CHEERING

He wasn't Joe DiMaggio the ballplayer anymore, but for the rest of his life, he was Joe DiMaggio the icon.

Some ballplayers hang around the only game they know as a manager or coach; most drift into the obscurity of real jobs in the real world. The great DiMaggio did neither. Instead, his job was remaining the great DiMaggio wherever he went, whatever he did. He even magnified his mystique when he married America's sex goddess, Marilyn Monroe, on January 14, 1954, in his hometown, San Francisco. During their honeymoon in Japan, she was asked to make a quick visit to American military personnel in nearby South Korea. On her return, she gushed, "Joe, you never heard such cheering."

"Yes, I have," the great DiMaggio said.

And he would hear more cheering. But after only nine months, only 274 days, they were divorced. "Her career was first," Dominic DiMaggio told *Sports Illustrated* after his brother's death. "Joe could not condone the things that Marilyn had to do. Joe wanted a wife he could raise children with. She could not do that. Joe had wanted that relationship to work. He held on to it for the rest of his life." When Monroe died at age 36 of an overdose of barbiturates on August 4, 1962, Joe took charge of the funeral arrangements. For the next 20 years, he had roses placed at her crypt three times a week.

His love for her evolved into his silence. If somebody mentioned her to him, that ended the conversation, if it didn't end whatever relationship existed with that person. And he certainly was not about to exploit his love for her in an autobiography.

In his life after baseball, Joe DiMaggio's job was being Joe DiMaggio. He visited military bases for a food company that supplied those

After his retirement, Joe DiMaggio did television commercials for "Mr. Coffee."

bases. He did television commercials as "Mr. Coffee" and for the Bowery Savings Bank in New York. When the baseball memorabilia craze developed, he commanded a six-figure fee for a weekend of signing baseballs, bats, uniforms and photos in his careful, flowing penmanship. That memorabilia-show income reportedly boosted his eventual estate to more than $50 million.

But other than a brief fling with the Oakland Athletics as a batting coach, the great DiMaggio remained a Yankee, the feature attraction of their annual Old-timers' Day.

The earthquake that interrupted the 1989 World Series in San Francisco also damaged his

Joe DiMaggio frequently attended the team's annual Old-timers' Day. In 1974 he joined Mickey Mantle, Yogi Berra, Whitey Ford and Casey Stengel at Yankee Stadium.

home in the Marina District there. When he resettled in Hollywood, Florida, his name raised millions of dollars for the Joe DiMaggio Children's Hospital, where the motto is "Whether rich or poor, no child is turned away." Sadly, he was estranged from his only child, Joe Jr., a Yale dropout who served in Vietnam. Joe and his first wife, Dorothy Arnold, divorced in 1945 and little Joe preferred his mother to his father.

"That was the end of it," Dominic DiMaggio said. "Joe Jr. said repeatedly, 'If my father calls for me, I will come.' But I know my brother. He would not do that. If Joe Jr. would have called his father, my brother would have accepted him with open arms."

Joe Jr. later suffered from drug abuse. Occasionally he was homeless. At the time of his father's death in 1999, he was found living in a battered trailer not far from San Francisco. He was a pallbearer at his father's funeral, but five

months later he died at 57 from an overdose of heroin and crack.

With an estranged son, the loves of the great DiMaggio's life were his two granddaughters, Paula and Cathy, and four great-grandchildren, Vanessah, Kendall, Valerie and Mitchell.

"I'm always thinking, what can I do for them, what can I get for them?" he said not long before he died. "I like to get them the newest computers. I'm big on education."

In his final years, the great DiMaggio, with a pacemaker in his heart, lived alone in a Harbour Island home in Hollywood, Florida. He had a white Mercedes-Benz, a gift from the Yankees, but he preferred to drive a gray Toyota Corolla. Although no longer strong enough to play golf, he often went to his nearby country club for a steam bath.

"He cooks for himself," his attorney Morris Engelberg said. "He pumps his own gas. He shines his own shoes."

Joe DiMaggio and Joe Jr. in happier times in 1947. The two had a fragile
relationship throughout their lives.

Joe DiMaggio signed thousands of items, but he didn't collect many himself.

For all the thousands of memorabilia items the great DiMaggio signed, he didn't collect many himself.

"I have baseballs autographed by Presidents Nixon, Ford, Carter and Bush," he told me in the late summer of 1998. "Another ball autographed by both President Reagan and Russia's Mikhail Gorbachev at a White House dinner I was invited to. And I still have the sterling silver humidor the players gave me for the hitting streak."

Those players were the 1941 teammates of the Yankee who basked in the cheering he always heard at the Stadium.

"I love doing it," he said, alluding to his appearances there at the World Series and Old-timers' Day. "It's like saying 'Hello' to the people. They love me and I love them. I love New York City."

Joe DiMaggio basked in the cheering he always heard at Yankee Stadium.

Part Three
MANTLE, MARIS
AND THE 1960s

By Robert Lipsyte

THE BABE was dead and Joe D was fading fast. The Brooklyn Dodgers, the Yankees' most frequent World Series rival, had seized national attention and the moral high ground by integrating baseball with the signing of Jackie Robinson. The postwar middle-class generation, the first with leisure and the money to enjoy it, was discovering the joys of golf, family travel, the backyard. Just winning wasn't enough in the springtime of the American Dream. The nation was primed for a new sports hero, one who reflected its bursting confidence in a boundless future.

Into this blaze of expectation—which he would never satisfy—came the golden teenager from the Old Indian Territory. He had Popeye forearms and a country-fresh grin. He was a switch-hitting slugger with dazzling speed. Even his name made us smile—Mickey Mantle.

This was the Yankees' hinge year, 1951. It was Mantle's rookie season and DiMaggio's last and Casey Stengel's third as manager, the one in which he solidified his hold on a locker room and a press box that had considered him a clown. Now he was regarded as the canny prime minister of the most powerful dynasty in sports history. Over an 18-year period, from 1947 through 1964, the Yankees would win an incredible 15 American League pennants and 10 World Championships.

And then it would be over, and the Yankees would nose-dive into the second division, losing more games than they won. The 22-year period

from 1951 until 1973, from the arrival of Mickey Mantle to the arrival of George Steinbrenner, was the miniseries version of the Rise and Fall of the Yankee Empire. The Bombers would rise again, of course, with their new owner and new heroes,

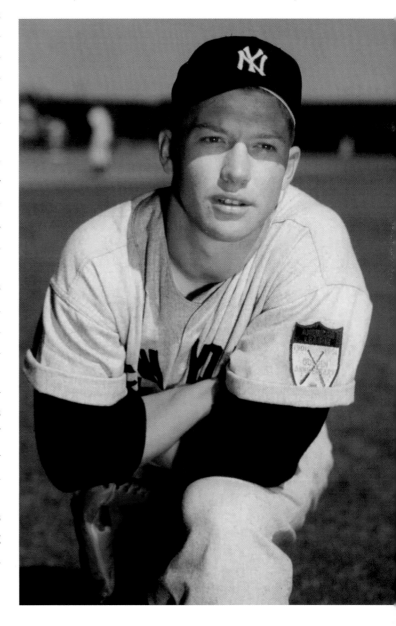

Mickey Mantle in spring training in 1951, at the age of 19.

Yogi Berra was a masterful catcher and great hitter who was confident enough to allow himself to be portrayed as a buffoon.

but never again with such a sense of imperial power. Yankee fans looked smug and Yankee haters said that rooting for the New York Yankees was like rooting for U.S. Steel.

But the team on the field was never the stereo-typed corporate machine of the fifties run by heartless men in gray flannel suits. Inside those pinstripes (really chalkstripes, said some tailors) was a diverse collection of personalities united by a tradition of excellence and an intimidating aura.

What else could unite "The Greatest Living Ballplayer," as the aloof DiMaggio would contrac-tually insist on being introduced; "The Scooter," Phil Rizzuto, the gabby little shortstop, whose real or affected fear of small animals made him the loveable butt of locker-room pranks; Yogi Berra, a masterful catcher and nonpareil bad-ball hitter confident enough to allow himself to be

portrayed as a buffoon; the slick Whitey Ford; the volatile Billy Martin; Roger Maris, the wrong hero in the right time; the willful-ly misinterpreted Ol' Perfesser Stengel; Jim Bouton, whose book "Ball Four" helped signal the end of this Yankee era as well as the end of a certain era of innocence; and above all the prodigiously talented, flawed and wounded Mick.

Perhaps Mantle reflected the country, which for all its super-powerhood nursed wrenching pain and dark secrets. America had won World War II yet was mired in a "police action" in Korea. We had shown the world that democracy triumphs, yet spooked ourselves with a lunatic search for suspected Communist traitors. The war had seemingly brought a fragmented nation together, yet there were already portents of the turbulence to come over racial justice, the Vietnam War and women's rights.

Even baseball was going to be turned upside down. In 1970 outfielder Curt Flood would insti-tute a lawsuit to prevent the St. Louis Cardinals from selling him to the Philadelphia Phillies. He would lose at the Supreme Court but the national pastime would never be the same; a few years later, two other players won the battle for free agency. Rich teams would be the greatest benefi-ciaries, and few were richer than the Yankees.

But in the spring of 1951, baseball was talking about Mantle, an Oklahoma lead miner's boy of such prodigious talent that he was getting a seri-ous look over after only one full season of pro ball—in Class C no less. There was some politics in his opportunity. Stengel, the sly "Ol' Perfesser" (he had actually held that title briefly as a college coach), was trying to purge the Yankees of the recalcitrant old guard players and restock the team with his own youngbloods. Part of it was ego and control, part rebuilding and part his philosophy that fundamentals counted ("Most ballgames are lost, not won," he liked to say). Younger players were more likely to participate enthusiastically in his two-a-day running, throwing and fielding drills.

Mantle was a willing student, this shy, 19-year-old hayseed who turned into a superman on the field. He had breathtaking speed on the basepaths and an awesome swing from either side of the plate. Veterans stopped to watch him take batting practice. He had come up as a shortstop, but Stengel was determined to play him in the outfield even though the Yankees were rich with such outfielders as Hank Bauer, Gene Woodling and Jackie Jensen. The general manager, George Weiss, wanted to let Mantle marinate in the minors for another year. Stengel wanted to keep him with the big club.

With Mantle's obvious gifts and his backstory, there was no way the press wouldn't clamor for him in New York. He was easy to write about and he was white; the pastime was beginning to darken with that first wave of African American stars—Robinson was followed by Larry Doby, Satchel Paige and Roy Campanella, among others, and the Giants just across the river were known to be grooming a phenomenal minorleaguer named Willie Mays.

Mantle was a fifth-generation American of English, German and Dutch lineage. His dad, Elvin, known as Mutt, a failed tenant farmer, had

Mickey Mantle was a willing student, a shy hayseed who turned into a superman on the field.

Mickey Mantle and teammate, Cliff Mapes, center, visiting Mantle's father, Elvin "Mutt," at a mine in Oklahoma in the summer of 1951. Mutt named his son after Mickey Cochrane, the Hall of Fame catcher.

raised his brood in tin-roofed shacks as he worked up from shoveler to boss in the mines.

Mutt was baseball-mad, a local diamond hero who named his son after Mickey Cochrane, the Hall of Fame catcher. By the time Mickey was four years old, Mutt was pitching to him every day before dinner. Mutt had a baseball mind. He foresaw platooning, a strategy Stengel would refine, in which left-handed batters would be sent up to face right-handed pitchers, and vice-versa. Mutt bribed Mickey with the cupcake left over in his lunch pail to practice swinging lefty, which Mickey hated.

But it was his mother who saved him for the big leagues. Despite Mutt's misgivings, Mickey played high school football. He was, no surprise, a good running back. During one practice during his sophomore year, he was kicked hard in the shin, and within a day he had a 104-degree temperature and a badly swollen leg. He spent two

weeks in the local community hospital. Lancing, liniments, sulfur didn't help. Finally, the doctor said that the bone was deeply abscessed. Osteomyelitis had set in. There was a chance they would have to amputate the leg.

It was Lovell Mantle who found the lawyer to draw up papers for her son to go to the Crippled Children's Hospital in Oklahoma City as a welfare patient. That year's medical miracle, penicillin, administered around the clock for several days, saved the leg and the career.

It was stories like these that burnished the halo around Mickey's already fair-haired head. While he was never as big as he was listed in Yankee yearbooks (when he arrived he was about 165 pounds and five feet, ten inches tall), his shoulders and arms were unusually powerful. He said they developed during his days as a "screen ape," breaking up boulders with a 16-pound sledgehammer.

Even more compelling was the shadow of doom over his family; cancer and other diseases ran in the genes and no male member of his family had ever lived past the age of 39. His apologists would offer this as explanation for his heavy drinking. He would later say he was drowning his homesickness.

The well-known Yankee scout Tom Greenwade signed Mickey on the day of his high school graduation, making him miss the ceremony so he could audition at one more game. Greenwade told Mutt that Mickey seemed small, his throwing arm weak, his play at shortstop erratic, but the Yankees were willing to take a risk. He offered Mickey $400 a month to play the rest of the summer in Class D. When Mutt hesitated, Greenwade sighed and threw in an $1,100 signing bonus.

Mantle remembered reading the announcement of his signing; Greenwade was quoted as saying Mantle would set records. For the rest of his life, Greenwade said Mantle was the best prospect he ever saw.

Despite the hype or maybe because of it, the great DiMaggio never gave Mickey the time of day when he arrived with the big club in 1951. It took a while for him to figure out it was the Clipper's way. Mantle's first time in the outfield, he flipped down sunglasses he had never used before to track a ball coming out of a bright sky.

Joe DiMaggio never gave Mickey Mantle the time of day when he arrived at spring training in 1951.

Everything went black and the ball hit him on the head. Nevertheless, he had a great spring.

But the regular season turned sour. Some of it was his fault; although Mantle was willing to work hard on his fielding in the new position and on his erratic throwing, something always kept him from totally applying himself, from mining his own talent. He reacted poorly to criticism, turning surly and getting down on himself. When he started off poorly, he withdrew into a shell.

"I got into trouble with the press early because I was scared," he said, years later. "I was young when I came to New York and got misquoted; well, maybe not so much misquoted as it came out not sounding like me talking. I was scared and I didn't really know how to handle it, so if you misquoted me, I just wouldn't talk to anybody, which made the whole joint mad." Crowds, reacting to his hype and attitude, booed him. Sportswriters wondered in print how he could be healthy enough to play baseball and not serve his country. Bleacher bums called him "draft dodger" and, "coward" and, perhaps the worst epithet of the 50s, "Commie."

The Yankees sent him to Oklahoma City for yet another draft physical. He was still 4-F; the osteomyelitis was still in his bones. But the criticism continued. Hurt, confused, he started dropping flyballs. He was batting only .269. In June, Stengel sent him down to the Yankees' minor-league team in Kansas City to regain his confidence. But he still couldn't hit.

In a story he loved to tell to generations of audiences that loved to hear it, Mantle called his father at the mines (the family had no home phone) and announced he was going to quit. Mutt ordered his son to stay put, jumped in his car and drove five hours to Kansas City. He burst into Mickey's hotel room. As he told it, Mantle said to his father, "Ah, Dad, listen, I tried as hard as I

could. And what for? Where am I headed? I'm telling you it's no use, and that's all there is to it. Hey, what are you doing?"

Mutt was furiously throwing his son's clothes into his cardboard suitcase. "I'm taking you home. I thought I raised a man, not a coward."

Shocked, Mickey pleaded, "Give me another chance. I'll try; honest I will."

Mutt relented. "What the hell. Why not?"

In the hotel coffee shop, Mutt told his boy, "So you've had your slump. Everybody has them, even DiMaggio. Take my word, it'll come together." And, of course, it did. Mantle stroked five hits in his next game, including two homers, and soon raised his minor-league batting average to .361. Stengel brought him back in August. Gil McDougald beat him out for Rookie of the Year honors, but Mantle was on the team, in right-field alongside DiMaggio, and he started in the World Series.

The Giants had reached that Series when Bobby Thomson hit his famously baseball-centric "Shot Heard Round the World" to beat the Dodgers in the last game of a best-of-three play-off and take the National League pennant.

At the start of the Series, according to "The Mick," the lively authorized 1985 biography by Herb Gluck, Stengel told Mantle, "Take everything you can get over in center. The Dago's heel is hurting pretty bad."

In the sixth inning of the second game, Mantle shaded toward center as the Giants' rookie sensation, Willie Mays, came to the plate. The right-handed Mays hit a high pop fly into short right-center. Remembering Stengel's instructions, Mantle sprinted toward the ball.

Although it would be many years before Mantle blamed the Clipper, others accused the vain and selfish DiMaggio for taking his time calling for the ball until he was absolutely sure he

On a ball hit by Willie Mays in Game 2 of the 1951 World Series, Mickey Mantle caught his spikes on a drain hole and stopped short, allowing Joe DiMaggio to make the catch. His leg was never the same after the accident.

could get to it. Once DiMaggio did yell, "I got it," Mantle stopped short. His spikes caught on the rubber cover of a drain hole dug into the outfield. He heard a "pop." Mantle went down so fast people thought he had been shot. He remembered looking up to see DiMaggio kneeling at his side, telling him not to move, that a stretcher was on its way. Mantle's leg was wrapped and splinted. The next day, Mutt, who had come to New York for the Series, took him to Lenox Hill Hospital. Climbing out of the cab on crutches, Mickey leaned on his father, who crumpled to the sidewalk.

They watched the Series together in adjoining

hospital beds, as Mickey's knee was operated on for torn ligaments. Steel weights were attached to the bottom of his cast. He was supposed to exercise the leg all winter, adding weight as it healed and grew stronger. In his typically self-destructive pattern, Mantle did not follow doctor's orders, and his leg never fully regained its strength. His speed was diminished. Mutt never got well at all; He had Hodgkin's Disease and died the following May. By then, Mickey had married Merlyn, a local girl Mutt had picked out for him, bought his family its first real house (with its own phone) and was on his way to taking over center field.

Ah, center field, the stage for worship and debate in New York in those glorious baseball years when there were three contending major-league teams in New York and each had a great centerfielder. Arguing over their relative merits was one way of arguing for the Dodgers of Brooklyn, the Giants of Manhattan or the Yankees of the Bronx.

Duke Snider was a powerful left-handed hitter who could field his position, although he probably couldn't run or throw with Mantle or Willie Mays, who some people feel was the best of the three, the greatest all-around ballplayer in history. But for all the Duke's powerful grace and Willie's flat-out "Say Hey" exuberance, Mickey was the one who captured the imagination. His statistical numbers—536 home runs, 16 All-Star Game appearances, 10 seasons batting over .300—do not begin to suggest the hopeful possibilities that sprang forth every time he swaggered to the plate.

Would he delicately drop a bunt and beat it out with a sprinter's speed? Would he blast the ball into orbit, once again sending it farther than a

The Yankees and Giants line up before Game 1 of the 1951 World Series at Yankee Stadium.

Whitey Ford won 236 games, lost 106 and struck out 1,956 batters in 16 seasons with the team.

star, babe magnet, door opener (if not always the instigator) of one of the sports world's most famous trio of bad boys. Mickey may have been a bumpkin when he first hit New York. Much of his drinking and carousing may, as he later claimed to sympathetic interviewers, have been an antidote to dislocation in the cold canyons of the city. But he clearly potentiated the street-savvy wildness of Whitey and Billy.

Edward Charles Ford, born in Manhattan and raised in Queens, was the son of a bartender and a grocery store clerk. He was a good-hitting high school first baseman when Yankee scout Paul Krichell suggested he concentrate on pitching. That summer, he pitched his sandlot team to the city championship, striking out 16 and scoring the winning run in a 1–0 game. The Yankees signed him for a $7,000 bonus, another good deal. A minor-league coach, the old Yankee pitcher Lefty Gomez, dubbed him "Whitey" for his hair.

Ford opened his rookie season, 1950, as a reliever, but talked Stengel, who always admired his brash confidence, into letting him start. Ford won his first nine games in a row. He won the fourth game of the World Series to polish off the Phillies, then went off to two years of military service. He came back in 1953 to win 18 and a new nickname, "Slick," from Stengel. It may have been for his almost supernatural coolness in clutch situations or from the term "Whiskey Slick," which the manager used to describe drunks who thought they were sober.

For all his good times, Ford must have picked his spots; in 16 Yankee seasons he won 236 games, lost 106 and struck out 1,956 batters. He probably would have won even more than that club record if Stengel hadn't tended to save him for critical games against tough clubs. He won 10 World Series games. Toward the end of his career, he scuffed the ball and applied dirt and

ball had ever been hit before? Would he be walked by a pitcher afraid to challenge him? Would he strike out with such forceful abandon that we knew, we just knew, that next time he would absolutely crush the ball?

Mantle quickly took his place in a team of tough professionals, none of them superstars, who could appreciate a phenom. For starters, he could win games for a powerful pitching staff that included the wily left-hander Ed Lopat, the powerful Vic Raschi and "Superchief" Allie Reynolds, a Native American who pitched two no-hitters in Mantle's rookie year. It didn't take too many seasons before the Yankees were Mantle's team. There was also a team within the team. Mickey was clearly the central figure, as

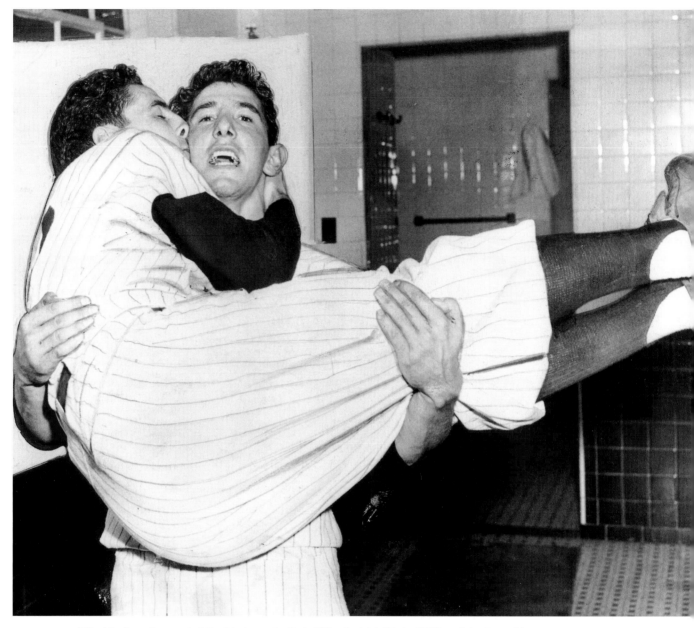

Billy Martin, who carried the Yankees to their fifth straight title in 1953, celebrates with
Phil Rizzuto after defeating the Dodgers in the World Series.

"foreign substances," to improve his curve.

"We sure had fun," Whitey told author Peter Golenbock in the seventies. He went on to describe a hunting trip in Texas. The three boys were in a 1930 Model-T convertible when they spotted a deer. Mickey and Billy jumped out while Whitey stayed perched on the top of the rumble seat.

"They were about five feet apart, Billy on my left, Mickey on my right, and I stayed in the seat, and I fired right between them. Pow! I aimed and shot right between their heads. They hit the dirt, face first in opposite directions, like you see the guys do in war movies. They turned sheet white. Every time I think of that I shudder." Whitey grinned. "I almost wiped out the Yankee team."

The third member of the three amigos, three musketeers or three stooges, depending on your take, was Martin, Stengel's pet, "the big-nosed kid" (he would have it surgically reduced as soon as he could afford it). The father-and-son affection between the fatherless infielder and the childless manager had taken seed in the minors and bloomed in New York. Billy was tough, cocky and a master of what is now called "small ball," the bunt, the hit-and-run, the surprise tactic. Billy came up in 1950 and was the regular second baseman by 1952, starring in two World Series before he left for the Army. He returned in time to help Ford and Mantle find trouble.

Mickey and Whitey made it into the Hall of Fame together in 1974. By that time, Billy was becoming more famous as a manager. Of the three, only Whitey lived a long and prosperous life. Billy died on Christmas Day, 1989, in a car accident. He may have been drunk at the time. Despite a liver transplant, Mickey died of cancer in 1995.

If there was any common denominator among Yankees in those days, it was skin color. The Yankees were among the last teams to integrate. Asked on a TV program in 1953 if he thought the Yankees were consciously discriminating, Jackie Robinson specifically blamed George Weiss, who was considered a bigot. Weiss insisted that he just hadn't found a player good enough for pinstripes; this in a time that included Robinson, Roy Campanella, Luke Easter, Minnie Minoso and Sam Jethroe, among others, dozens of Negro Leaguers who never got a major-league shot, and, most important, Vic Power and Ruben Gomez, who were languishing in the Yankee farm system. Gomez eventually bought back his contract and signed with the Giants, winning 13 games in 1953. Power was a black Puerto Rican with a flashy style that the Yankee publicity mill spun as "showboating" and "attitude." It was also said that he couldn't field. When Power finally made it

to the majors, he won seven Gold Gloves.

In 1955 the Yankees brought up 26-year-old Elston Howard, a consistent All-star who was named the American League's Most Valuable Player in 1963. Howard was dignified, proud to be a pioneer and willing to put up with segregation; he did not stay with the team at its spring training hotel in St. Petersburg, Florida, and he agreed when Weiss asked him to quietly skip the exhibition game against the Birmingham farm club.

Stengel's famous crack about Howard, usually reported as something like "When I finally get one, I get the only one who can't run," can be interpreted as a result of Stengel's bigotry, the casually expressed racism of the time or, most likely, another example of the old manager's offhanded nastiness. He could be cutting. Howard, who seemed to get along with everyone, was particularly grateful to the college-educated first baseman and slugger Moose Skowron, the hardbitten, hustling outfielder Hank Bauer and Phil Rizzuto, each of whom went out of his way to make the black rookie feel comfortable.

Howard was an outfielder the Yankees had turned into a catcher as Yogi Berra's backup; some writers thought it was a way of keeping him on the bench. He did not play full-time his first two seasons, but Stengel often platooned him in the outfield.

But in 1956, there might as well have been only one Yankee outfielder. In what would turn out to be his so-called Golden Season, Mantle won the triple crown—batting .353, hitting 52 home runs and batting in 130 runs. He won the first of his three Most Valuable Player Awards. And the Yankees beat the Dodgers in the last Subway Series of New York's three-team era.

That series was tied two games each when Don Larsen took the mound in the fifth game at the Stadium. Larsen, known to his teammates as

In 1955 the team brought up Elston Howard, a consistent All-star who was named Most Valuable Player in 1963. Here he enjoys a victory with Mickey Mantle and Hank Bauer.

"Gooney Bird," had made news in spring training by wrapping his car round a telephone pole at 5 A.M. No one was surprised. After all, his favorite expression was "Let the good times roll."

But his second front-page appearance, on October 8, *was* a surprise. Larsen had been knocked out in the second inning of the second game, which the Yankees lost. He was an inconsistent pitcher who came to the Yankees as part of an 18-player deal with the Orioles. He was a big, strong right-hander who never fulfilled his promise. Was he missing commitment, maturity, a fire in his belly? Stengel, in his often curt and cutting way, later said of him, "He should be good but he ain't."

But in the fifth game, he was perfect, dominating batters with a new pitching motion that he had refined late in the season. In his wonderful

Mickey Mantle won the triple crown in 1956—batting .353, hitting 52 home runs and batting in 130 runs. Here he bats against Don Ferrarese of Baltimore in May at Yankee Stadium.

history of the Yankees from 1949 to 1964, "Dynasty," Peter Golenbock describes it:

"Using his no-windup delivery, Larsen was pitching effortlessly. With his pitching hand in his glove, he would begin his delivery, hands together at chest height, leaning back on his left leg and then twirling the leg forward, using it as a whip before extending his right arm and delivering the pitch to the plate."

He did that 97 times, and his control was so fine that only once did he throw three balls to a batter. He threw 70 strikes.

There were few close calls, his command was overpowering and following baseball supersition, no one mentioned the possibility of a no-hitter. Teammates stayed away from him when he came back to the dugout. After seven innings, there was an exchange with Mantle that has a number of ver-

Don Larsen embraces Yogi Berra after Larsen pitched a perfect game against the
Dodgers in Game 5 of the 1956 World Series at Yankee Stadium.

sions. Larsen maintains in his 2001 memoir with Mark Shaw, "The Perfect Yankee," that he said to the Mick, "Look at the scoreboard! Wouldn't it be something? Two more innings to go."

Mantle stood up wordlessly and walked to the end of the bench.

Berra, who caught the game, offered a postgame commentary that gave some insight into the intelligence for which he rarely got credit. Larsen would never have pitched such a disciplined game, according to Berra, if the score had not been so close. At 9–0, for example, said Berra, Larsen would have lost concentration, gotten wild, grooved a few pitches. But with only a 2-run lead and the Series tied at two games each, he could not afford to get careless for even one pitch.

"At the start of the ninth," said Berra, "I didn't say a thing about how well he was throwing. I went to the mound and reminded him that if he walked one guy and the next guy hit one out the game was tied."

Afterward, recalling Larsen's one-car accident, Yankee owner Del Webb said, "This will set spring training back forever." Larsen, after receiving *Sport* magazine's award as the Series' most valuable player, a Corvette convertible, said, "I shouldn't have any trouble picking up girls in this thing."

The perfect year turned out to be more of a peak than a prelude for Larsen, the Yankees and Mantle.

The next year, 1957, the Copacabana year, would be the last season that the Dodgers, the Giants and Billy Martin would play in New York.

On May 15, after a 29th birthday dinner for

Mickey Mantle rounding third on a homer as he is escorted by fans on July 23, 1957. He also had a single, double and triple that day as he hit for the cycle against the White Sox.

Martin at Danny's Hideaway, a group including Johnny Kucks and his wife, the Bauers, the Berras, the Mantles and the Fords went to hear Johnny Ray sing his hit song, "Cry," at the Waldorf-Astoria, then on to the Copacabana to catch Sammy Davis Jr. A special table was set up for them close to the stage.

Unfortunately, the Yankee table was also close to a table of bowlers celebrating a league championship. One of the bowlers shouted a racial epithet at Davis, who stopped the band and sarcastically thanked him for it.

After Bauer told the bowlers to shut up, they began heckling the Yankees. Martin invited the bowlers to step out and meet him in the gutter. Mantle and Bauer followed to protect his back. A few minutes later, in the men's room, Yogi and Whitey were restraining Bauer, who was standing over a bowler with a broken nose. Later, Bauer swore he had never touched the man, although he had wanted to; a Copa bouncer had gotten to him first.

The *New York Post* entertainment columnist, Leonard Lyons, got the story and it was front-page news. Yankee management levied $1,000 fines, substantial amounts in those days, even before the players appeared before a grand jury. According to Mantle, when he was asked what happened to the bowler in the bathroom, he said, "I think Roy Rogers rode through the Copa on his horse and Trigger kicked that man in the head."

The grand jury laughed and the case was dismissed for insufficient evidence.

But the players never forgave the club for its rush to judgment, which also colored the attitude of the press and the public. These Yankees were rowdy drunks, not men taking their wives out for a night on the town.

And then a month later, in Chicago, Art Ditmar threw a head-hunting fastball at White Sox slug-

ger Larry Doby, who sprawled in the dirt. When the pitch got past Elston Howard, Ditmar ran in to cover the plate. Doby supposedly threatened Ditmar that he'd stick a knife in the pitcher's back if he ever did that again. Punches were thrown and both benches cleared.

Once the umpires had the melee under control, Martin asked Ditmar what Doby had said. Enraged, Martin charged Doby and began pummelling him. Doby, Walt Dropo and Enos Slaughter were thrown out of the game. Martin was traded to Kansas City a few days later. Weiss had never liked him, and now he had an excuse to get rid of him despite Stengel's objections. Also, the 21-year-old Bobby Richardson was ready to play second base regularly. Clean-living and religious, Richardson and Tony Kubek had once confounded Weiss's private dicks by leading them out at night to a YMCA Ping-Pong match.

Mickey and Whitey cried in the locker room when Billy was traded. Martin, angry, didn't talk to Stengel for years. "I needed Casey only one time in my life and he let me down," said Martin.

Casey simply couldn't protect his wild boy anymore. And by 1960, Casey himself was on the way out, even though he once again won the pennant. Although Casey's age was the reason he was fired, it was a decision he made at the start of the World Series that was used by the owners to prove he had lost it.

Stengel and his pitching coach, Ed Lopat, started Art Ditmar in the first game against the Pittsburgh Pirates rather than Ford, their ace. Ditmar lost that game as well as the fifth. Ford won the third and the sixth, by shutouts. That rotation meant that the left-hander was unavailable for the seventh game, which Pittsburgh won in the bottom of the ninth on Bill Mazeroski's home run.

Five days later, the Yankees held a press con-

Hank Bauer, second from right, of the New York Yankees, stands with his wife, Charlene, and teammate Mickey Mantle, far left, and ex-teammate Billy Martin outside the New York City Criminal Courts building after a grand jury cleared Bauer of felonious assault charges on June 24, 1957. The players appeared before a grand jury who returned a "no bill" on the charge that Bauer beat a New York delicatessen operator in the Copacabana nightclub in May, during a birthday party for Martin, who was recently traded to the Kansas City Athletics.

ference to announce that Stengel was leaving. Dan Topping avoided saying that Stengel had resigned or quit, but talked about his participation in a profit-sharing plan.

Stengel read a speech that had been prepared for him, then rambled around the subject until a reporter asked him directly if he had been fired.

"Write anything you want," he snapped. "Quit, fired, whatever you please. I don't care."

Later, he added, "I'll never make the mistake of being seventy again."

Two weeks later, his old pal and boss George Weiss was fired, too. He was 65. There was little

sympathy for Weiss, the cold, shy Yalie who had run the club as a paternalistic dictatorship, keeping salaries low to maximize his own profits while offering loans and paying emergency doctor bills to engender gratitude and keep control. At the formal announcement of his leaving, he amazed reporters by crying. His life had been the Yankees. He also knew that the club would soon be hurting as much as he was; the talent pipeline was going dry.

"The Yankees have five more years at the most under the new management," he said.

It turned out to be four years. But even the

Ralph Houk, nicknamed "Major," managed the Yankees from 1961 to 1963 with two World Championships.

brilliant Weiss couldn't foresee the good news—within two years he and Stengel would be returning triumphantly to baseball.

The owners had dumped Casey for Ralph Houk, the 41-year-old former backup catcher whom Casey had kept on to coach. Houk was smart, aggressive and relentlessly sunny, never criticizing a player in public, always finding a shred of hope in a bad loss. Players liked him. He was tough, but accessible. The owners were afraid he would leave before Stengel did. Houk had earned his nickname "Major" in combat duty during World War II. When a newsman asked him if any part of managing made him nervous, he laughed and said, "Why, is someone going to be shooting at me?" He had perspective.

Houk would be the right commander for the 1961 season, famous for Maris breaking Babe Ruth's single-season home run record, less well-known for showcasing a Yankee team second only to the immortals of 1927. It would be the last great Yankee team for a long time.

The infield was strong; Moose at first, Richardson at second, Kubek at short and Clete Boyer at third led the league with 180 double plays. Skowron and Kubek were All-star selections, along with the entire outfield—Maris, Mantle and the fading but still productive Berra—the pitchers Ford and Luis Arroyo, and the catcher, Howard.

Long before the season started, Houk made an off-hand comment that in retrospect seemed clairvoyant. Speaking of Mantle, he said, "If he hits sixty homers and Maris hits fifty-nine, they'll make me a hell of a manager."

But the 28-year-old Mantle was out of public favor. Fans were booing him regularly, and in an incident rare in those days, a man jumped out of the stands in Yankee Stadium, raced across center field and punched Mantle in the face. Mantle was seen drinking his meals for a few days. Insiders snickered, What else is new?

Tony Kubek crosses home plate after a homer and is greeted by Moose Skowron and Mickey Mantle. The three would add to a strong 1961 team, the last great Yankee team for a long time.

Luis Arroyo, Yankee reliever, waiting for
the call from the bullpen in 1961.

But relief was on its way. Roger Maris joined the Yankees in 1960. When he broke in with the Cleveland Indians in 1957, a local sportswriter tagged him "a future Mickey Mantle." His rookie year might even have borne out that promise if it hadn't ended prematurely with two broken ribs, an injury characteristic of his unselfish, flat-out style. He was hurt trying to break up a double play.

And now this poker-faced 25-year-old with a bristly crew cut and a matter-of-fact Midwestern tone was in right field alongside the Mick. The two powered the club to another American League pennant. Mantle hit 40 home runs in 1960 and Maris hit 39, and was selected Most Valuable Player. Maris's career statistics with four teams over 12 years—275 homers, 851 runs batted in, a .260 average—don't quite do him justice. Maris was a fine fielder with a strong, accurate arm,

Roger Maris was also a fine outfielder with a strong, accurate arm. Here he robs Ken Hunt of the Los Angeles Angels of a homer in 1961 at Yankee Stadium.

and was a fast, bold base runner. He basked in the fellowship of the locker room where he was considered a decent, hard-working, talented regular guy.

But he wasn't the Mick—who wasn't the Mick either. Fans were tired of waiting for him to become the new Joe D, much less the new Babe Ruth.

And then it was 1961.

"That's when people starting liking me," said Mickey in the eighties. "After Roger beat me in the home-run race, I could do no wrong. Everywhere I went I got standing ovations. All I had to do was walk out on the field. Hey, what the hell? It's a lot better than having them boo you."

We were drinking in an Atlantic City hotel where he did public relations. His shrug was typically endearing and cynical at the same time. "I became the underdog; they hated him and liked me. He was pitched into the middle of all this publicity. We used to have more sportswriters following us that year than we had baseball players. All of a sudden it was on top of him, it was tough. That's why I think it was such a great thing he did, beating Babe Ruth's record."

But the world didn't think so and laconic, jut-jawed Maris, the son of a North Dakota railroad man, never could figure out why. He did exactly what a baseball player was supposed to do, and people hated him for it.

No one expected him to break the record, including Maris. He was considered the rabbit, the pacesetter who would lead Mantle into a hot, streaky September, then fade as the Mick went long. As Maris remembered it to me, the pressure was all on Mantle while he just had to give a few more smiles and autographs.

But it was Mantle who faded. By the second week in September, Maris had 56 home runs and Mantle had 53 with 18 games remaining. Mantle had a bad head cold; he felt sore and stiff. A friend sent him to a well-known Dr. Feelgood who gave him an amphetamine injection which caused an abscess on his hip. He was hospitalized and hit only one more homer that season.

In 1984, a year before he died of cancer, Roger Maris said: "You know, 1961 was an easy season. It was fun. It was exciting. How could it not be? But what happened afterward, well, it still bitters me up to talk about it."

Later books, and Billy Crystal's movie, "61*," made the experience seem far more wearing than Maris chose to remember it. In retrospect, neither are wrong; the portents of the later "bitters" were adding up and Maris may have been in necessary denial.

The pressures and pettiness that would dog the rest of Maris's Yankee career had begun. Sportswriters complained that Maris wasn't "Ruthian" enough to break the sacred mark. He was also not quotable enough. Thus, every Maris move was interpreted through his "unworthiness."

Soon, he could do nothing right. He had hit 54 homers—he was 3 ahead of Mickey at the time—when he came to bat with Kubek on third. The infield was deep for the slugger. Maris dropped a perfect bunt, which he beat out as Kubek scored. Later, when sportswriters asked why he had bunted, he said, "We still have a pennant to win."

Had Mantle said that, he would have been praised as an unselfish player who put the team above himself. Maris was put down for answering in a cold and disdainful way.

When he hit No. 57, in Detroit, it bounced back onto the field. Al Kaline threw it to Maris as a souvenir. When the pack of writers asked Maris afterward if he appreciated Kaline's gesture, Maris answered, in his signature no-nonsense truthfulness, "Well, any of the players would have done that." It was seen as surly, ungrateful Maris knocking a nice guy. Sportswriters were creating the image of Maris as a time bomb.

When Commissioner Ford Frick, who had been Babe Ruth's ghostwriter, announced that if Ruth's record was broken after the Yankees' 154th game—the length of that 1927 season—it might be necessary to have *two* records, few writers pointed out that Ruth had never had to play at night or fly. The folklore evolved to having Frick declare that an asterisk would be attached (it never did). Maris's edgy relations with the press corps, swelling daily like some alien life form, worsened as he sensed its hostility. His hair began to fall out.

After Mantle, stalled at 53 homers, realistically conceded that he had no chance to break the

No one expected Roger Maris to break Babe Ruth's home run record, including Roger Maris. Here Maris stands next to Babe's plaque in the monument area of the outfield at Yankee Stadium on September 10, 1961.

record within 154 games, Maris was asked for comment. He was typically honest: "Mickey shouldn't concede. He's too good a competitor to concede." The stories in which that quote appeared interpreted Maris as knocking Mantle. Maris decided he wasn't going to give any more interviews.

In the next city on that road trip, trapped by the pack outside the trainer's room, Maris shouted,

"I don't want to talk about the record. What do you want? You want me to concede? Okay, I concede. All right?" He stormed away.

Ballplayers sympathized with Maris and rooted for him, but most sportswriters were thinking only of their stories, not about a young man under pressure. He became a certified target. All the journalists who had been afraid to reveal that Mantle could be mean and crabby, not to mention drunk, now went after Roger as a complainer, a whiner, a pop-off.

It had always been Mantle who brushed off autograph-seekers, who turned his back on reporters with a casual curse, while Maris stood and signed and thoughtfully answered questions. But it was Mantle who now got the good ink and Maris who got the side-effects of a bad press—chairs, half-filled bottles, nuts and bolts, thrown from the stands.

"It drove me into somewhat of a shell," said Maris. "I just didn't enjoy being in the ballpark like I did. I mean, it's almost like going into a snake pit."

The Yankees' 154th game was in Baltimore and Maris was a mess. He was in Houk's office, in tears, asking the manager if he could sit out the game.

In a book he wrote with Robert W. Creamer, "Season of Glory," Houk recalled saying, "Look, Roger, why don't you go out and hit in batting practice and let me put you in the lineup. You start the game and after an inning or two, I'll take you out if you want. We can say you're sick."

Roger stayed in the game, hit his 59th homer, and the Yankees clinched the pennant. It was the biggest moment so far in Houk's career. There was a small celebration, mostly unnoticed by the press. Maris, pinned by reporters to a clubhouse wall, finally seemed relaxed.

He matched Ruth's 60 in the 158th game in Baltimore. On October 1, in the fourth inning of the last game, the 162nd, he slammed a Tracy Stallard fastball into the the right-field stands at Yankee Stadium for No. 61.

Phil Rizzuto, by then a broadcaster, cried, "Holy Cow! He did it."

That should have been the end of it. The phantom asterisk never actually appeared, and Maris was generally accepted as the man who broke the Babe's record. The Yanks went on to win the World Series against the Cincinnati Reds, capping Manager Houk's rookie season. He started Whitey Ford in the first game, and the left-hander won that game and the fourth. Maris hit only one homer in five games, Mantle none.

But the snakes didn't stop hissing. In spring training, a reporter asked, "Will you hit 62 in 1962?" Maris stormed out.

And then it got worse. Oscar Fraley, the United Press International columnist who had written the stories that became "The Untouchables" on TV and movie screens, took off on Roger without actually interviewing him. Fraley wrote: "For a man who belabored the ball at a rather anemic .269 clip, I would have to think that Maris has a rather swollen idea of his importance. John Glenn . . . went for the circuit when it really counted . . . guys like Maris bat a round zero with me."

Boiling over that piece, Maris brushed off his old friend, the columnist Jimmy Cannon, who needed some spring training quotes. Maris snapped, "Later," as he rushed away, trying to control his fury.

Cannon, thin-skinned and famously grouchy himself, immediately wrote a two-part series in which he called his friend "a whiner . . . a thrilling freak." He compared him unfavorably to Mantle. He even revised his own 1961 reporting, calling himself "slovenly" for not "turning it on him for his treacherous smallness." He predicted that Maris would cause dissension on the club.

Coming from a nationally syndicated star like Cannon, it set a tone. How could anyone now write kindly about such a creep, record or not? It was a license for everyone who wanted to dump on Maris to do so, even if their only true motivation was their frustration at not being able to dump on Mantle.

By the end of 1961 Mickey Mantle was getting the good press and Roger Maris was getting the side-effects of bad ink—chairs, bottles, nuts and bolts, thrown from the stands.

Even though Roger Maris broke Babe Ruth's record while playing four more games than Ruth, Maris was generally accepted as the man who broke Babe's record.

Poor Maris was ready to go home.

Mantle and Maris would get to play in three more World Series, beating the Giants in 1962, losing to the Dodgers in 1963 and to the Cardinals in 1964. But it was the final years of the old Yankee empire. Everything began to change in 1962.

The athlete as masculine superstar became something of a cartoon when Colonel John Glenn, who had flown fighter missions over Korea with Ted Williams, became the first American to orbit the Earth.

The legend of Joe DiMaggio expanded when Marilyn Monroe died, reportedly of a sleeping pill overdose, and the Clipper stepped up to take charge of her funeral. The Hollywood and political friends, who he felt had killed her, were barred, and his order to leave a fresh rose on her grave, every day forever, touched romantic hearts. That order would eventually be rescinded, and gossipy books would tarnish his legend.

Of most impact on the Yankees was the new team in the city, the Mets. They were so enthusiastically welcomed by fans and sportswriters hungry for the return of the National League that their early incompetence was hailed. There was something anti-Yankee in that.

Roger Angell wrote in *The New Yorker* that the passion of Mets fans intimated "a new recognition that perfection is admirable but a trifle inhuman, and that a stumbling kind of semi-success can be much more warming." The player who became symbolic of of the Mets as the team set records for losing was the genial, bumbling Marv Throneberry. He had come up as a highly touted Yankee rookie in 1958 and played two seasons in the outfield alongside Mantle.

Meanwhile, the Yankees brought up what looked like a promising rookie class.

There was Tom Tresh, a switch-hitting shortstop, who batted .286 with 20 homers in 1962. He made the All-star Team and was the league's Rookie of the Year. He switched to the outfield, but was dogged by injuries and was traded in 1969. He soon retired.

There was Phil Linz, the so-called super sub who played the outfield and all the infield positions except first base over the next four years. He became best known for playing a harmonica in the back of the team bus after a loss on the road. He and Manager Berra got into a screaming match. Berra fined Linz $200 and a harmonica company gave him a $20,000 contract to help bring the instrument back into vogue. It seemed fitting that Linz finished his career with the Mets.

Bobby Richardson and Tom Tresh in 1962. Tresh made the All-star Team that year and was the league's Rookie of the Year.

The most talented of that rookie class was probably Brooklyn-born Joe Pepitone, so coveted by the Yankees that they signed him at age 18 for a reported $20,000 even after he was accidentally shot in the stomach by a friend showing off a new handgun. Pepitone characteristically blew the bonus on a car and speedboat.

He also blew his career, although that took longer. An excellent first baseman with power, an intense player and affable with fans, he simply couldn't give up his Saturday night fevers. He was

something of an exotic in that clubhouse, the first to show up with a blow-dryer and, as his natural hair disappeared, separate toupees for games and for partying. Mantle was particularly amused by Pepitone, even after he put washing-machine detergent in his whirlpool bath, and befriended him. When Pepitone was separated from his second wife, and broke, Mantle put him up in his hotel suite and fed him. Mantle also took him to parties, which he did not need. Pepitone, by his own admission, became a pet of Italian-American gangsters who supplied him with chicks and booze while exhorting him to "make us proud" as a great major leaguer. Eventually,

the candle burning at both ends melted.

The rookie who would ultimately have the most long-term influence was Bouton. In the controversy over "Ball Four," and his stormy career as a sportscaster and sitcom star, Bouton's early success is often forgotten. He was a fierce competitor dubbed by Mantle "a bulldog with stuff." Used mostly in relief in 1962, Bouton began pitching in the rotation in 1963. He won 21 regular-season games that year, and lost a 1–0 duel against Don Drysdale of the Dodgers in the World Series. In 1964 Bouton won 18 regular-season games, and two more in the World Series the Yankees lost to the Cardinals.

Phil Linz celebrating the Yankees' American League pennant victory with manager Yogi Berra in 1964. Linz and Berra had gotten into a screaming match over Linz playing a harmonica in the back of the team bus after a loss on the road earlier that season.

"I remember thinking," Bouton told Golenbock, "I didn't think it would be this easy. I would be in the Hall of Fame. I would be able to throw forever."

Fresh, smart, honest, socially conscious (rare for an athlete then, he campaigned for such human rights causes as the end of South African apartheid), Bouton became the favorite of a new generation of sportswriters called Chipmunks (named by the irascible Maris-basher, Jimmy Cannon, for their scurrying, chattery ways in the press box). It was one of the chief Chipmunks, Stan Isaacs of *Newsday*, who was credited with ushering in the New Age of sports journalism with a question to Ralph Terry after he won Game 5 of the 1962 World Series. Terry had been called away from the postgame press conference to take a call from his wife, who had recently given birth. The proud new dad returned to the newspack with the news that his wife was feeding his child.

Isaacs asked, "Breast or bottle?"

But for all the new journalism, the real breakthrough in sportswriting would come in 1970 with the publication of Bouton's memoir, written with Len Shecter. "Ball Four" was a valentine to baseball. Young major leaguers would later tell Bouton that they had opted for baseball over basketball because of the joy in that book. But Commissioner Bowie Kuhn and older sportswriters were appalled by its glimpses into the sanctum of the locker room. Only the commissioner and sportswriters were allowed to have that access.

Bouton has always suspected that the baseball establishment really hated the book for economic reasons; it revealed that baseball wages were low and that one way owners kept them low was by depriving players of information about profits and salaries. Bouton urged players to share information and ask for more money. While this

Joe Pepitone, an excellent first-baseman with power, was the first to use a blow-dryer in the clubhouse. He had separate toupees for games and partying.

seems simple-mindedly quaint by 21st-century standards, there were few agents in those days and no free agency, and the economics of baseball had yet to become part of the sports report.

But the official anti–"Ball Four" line was that suggestible youngsters should not be exposed to disclosures of the bad behavior of their role models.

Particularly appalling to the sycophants was a racy anecdote, also endearingly quaint now, about Mantle leading teammates to the roof of a Washington, D.C., hotel to spy on women getting undressed. It was called "beaver-shooting."

Bouton always seemed a little surprised and

Mickey Mantle with Jim Bouton in 1962. In Bouton's book, "Ball Four," he portrayed the light and dark sides of Mantle.

In "Ball Four," Bouton portrayed the light and dark sides of Mantle. Bouton recalled his first Yankee victory, in 1962. "When the game was over I walked back into the clubhouse and there was a path of white towels from the door to my locker, and all the guys were standing there, and just as I opened the door Mickey was putting the last towel in place. I'll never forget him for that.

"On the other hand, there were all those times when he'd push little kids aside when they wanted his autograph and the times he was snotty to reporters, just about making them crawl and beg for a minute of his time. I've seen him close a bus window on kids trying to get his autograph."

Of course, the pressure on Mantle never quit. In his final years, he ate all his meals in his hotel room. To go out was to be mobbed. Pepitone once dressed in black like a mob enforcer and spent a day growling people away from the Mick.

One young reporter got a glimmer of just how relentless was the assault on Mantle when he became the butt of a favorite Yankee joke. On the reporter's first road trip with the team, his hotel room number was given to groupies in the lobby as Mantle's. All night long, there were knocks on the reporter's door, and every time he opened it he was greeted with profound, soul-chilling disappointment.

Bouton hurt his arm in 1964, and although he came back strongly that year, the sore arm plagued him again in 1965 and never healed. His last Yankee season was 1968, as was Mantle's. By then, everyone had gotten old.

The shrewdest of baseball observers, Leonard Koppett, has written that "a sequence of historic events and bad decisions in 1964 changed the

sad that Mantle, who never read the book, was quoted as being angry at it. It would be many years, after both men buried children, before there was any contact.

"Mickey was a god among his teammates," said Bouton. "I remember on payday, when the traveling secretary brought our checks to the clubhouse, guys would wave the checks and say, 'Thanks, Mick.'

"Players respond to money and muscles, and Mick had both. We were always thinking up ways to describe how strong he was. I think the winner was Dale Long, who said, 'Mickey Mantle has muscles in his shit.'"

Right: The pressure on Mickey Mantle never quit. He was forced to eat meals in his hotel room because he would be mobbed if he went out.

course of baseball history, ending four decades of Yankee dominance."

Koppett names Dan Topping as "the instigator"; he was planning to sell his share of the club, without giving up operative control, and he wanted management with whom he was comfortable. So he bumped Houk, the combat field officer, up to headquarters as general manager, and he appointed Berra, who was still playing in 1963, as the dugout manager of his recent teammates.

Koppett's analysis blames Yankee hubris and greed for the moves. Berra was hired to counteract some of the enormous media attention that Stengel was drawing across town with the Mets; Yogi would just have to show up, say, "It ain't over till it's over" or "When you come to a fork in the road, take it," while the Yankees would win by themselves. They were so good, they didn't need a real manager. And if they ran into a snag, there was always Major Houk in the front office.

As it turned out, Berra was a far better manager than Topping gave him credit for, and the Yankees were a far worse team. But with Houk accessible, it was too easy for players to go over Yogi's head for stroking and pep talks, further reducing the new manager's authority.

Meanwhile, the minors were not producing that traditional flow of Yankee talent. Koppett blames that on Weiss. Realizing his reign was ending, the general manager had "started starving the farm system to maximize profits (in which he and other employees shared)." There was no fresh help as the Bombers began slipping behind the Orioles that summer.

In August, Topping and Webb sold 80 percent of the club to the Columbia Broadcasting System. Topping stayed on as president and decided to dump Berra at the end of the season. Houk suggested replacing him with Johnny Keane, manager

of the St. Louis Cardinals, who were also floundering that season.

Incredibly, both clubs rallied to win their pennants, and Keane and Berra met in the World Series. In a comic, bitter shuffle, Keane won the Series, was fired by the Cardinals and became the Yankee manager. Berra joined Stengel as a coach with the Mets.

Keane and most of the Yankee players never bonded. A thoughtful, religious man, he regarded his new team as lost souls with "careless habits." Yankees began calling him "Squeaky." It didn't help that the team was coming apart physically. Tony Kubek, the starting shortstop, had a bad back. Whitey Ford was recovering from surgery for a blocked artery in his pitching arm. Mantle's shoulder was hurting and he pulled a hamstring. Roger Maris broke his right hand. Elston Howard injured his arm. The Yankees finished with a 77–85 record, in sixth place. It was the team's worst showing in 40 years.

And then it got worse. The Yankees dropped into last place in the 1966 season. Keane was fired and Houk returned to the dugout, but this time he was managing a team of wounded old men. The farm system was ruined. There would be a few more bona fide stars emerging in the 60s—pitcher Mel Stottlemyre, who would have three 20-win seasons and become the pitching coach of the 90s' powerhouse; Bobby Murcer, the Yankees' best hitter in the early 70s; and Thurman Munson, the 1969 Rookie of the Year and a main reason for the Yankees' resurgence in the late seventies, who died piloting his own plane during the 1979 season—but the Bombers had bombed. Between the pillaging of the farm system in the late 50s and the arrogant refusal to mine the market when they had it to themselves, the club was hurting for prospects and customers. When it dumped Mel Allen, its most

Mel Stottlemyre, the team's pitching star of the 1960s, had three 20-game-winning seasons. Here he pitches to Jim Northrup of Detroit at Yankee Stadium.

recognizable radio voice, it lost a connection to its audience. Mike Burke, the urbane, long-haired, sociable executive from CBS, became the most quoted and sought-after Yankee.

Mantle's last season was 1968, and within a few years he seemed like history even to himself. In a poignant moment years later, he said, "Somebody asked me how I would like to be remembered, and the first thing I thought of is that I really believe that all the players that played with me liked me. Sometimes I sit in my den at home and read stories about myself. Kids used to save whole scrapbooks on me. They get tired of 'em and mail 'em to me. I must have seventy-five or eighty. I'll go in there and read 'em and you know what? They might as well be about Musial or DiMaggio. It's like reading about somebody else."

Bobby Murcer was the team's best hitter in the early 1970s.
Here he meets the fans on Bat Day in 1971.

In 1969, at a time of great turmoil in the country and particular unrest in the cities, after an exciting National League pennant race, the Mets won the World Series. Just half a dozen years earlier they were the worst team in baseball. Pundits found metaphors for hope and healing and rebirth.

It was not the worst time for the Yankees to be in hibernation. Baseball was overshadowed by the turbulence of the 60s. Muhammad Ali was stripped of his heavyweight championship for refusing to be drafted into the army in 1967. The most lasting image of the 1968 Mexico City Olympic Games was that of two American medal winners, Tommie Smith and John Carlos, raising black-gloved fists in the Black Power salute from the Olympic podium. The nation's First Fan, Richard Nixon, used the language of football to

Mickey Mantle believed that all the players that played with him liked him.
Here he gave outfield advice to Yogi Berra in 1958.

explain his foreign policy. Pro football was proclaiming itself the new national pastime.

In 1970 Curt Flood instituted his restraint-of-trade suit against baseball's so-called reserve clause, actually a labyrinth of rules that bound a player to the club that originally signed him. Flood's language in interviews—he called himself "a well-paid slave, but nevertheless a slave"—was mocked by sportswriters who

weren't making $90,000 a year, as was the Cardinals' outfielder. He lost his case before the Supreme Court, but his principled stance began the process that eventually led to more of a balance between employer and employee in sports.

When the Yankees finished in second place that year, Houk ordered champagne for the clubhouse. How pathetic: the descendents of Murderers' Row, celebrating being runners-up. It

Mike Kekich, left, has a sign on his locker reading "I'll get the last laugh." And Fritz Peterson shows him a sign reading, "We'll just see." The two exchanged wives, children and dogs in a "lifestyle" swap.

was their best finish since 1964 and Houk was named American League Manager of the Year, even though Baltimore had run off with the pennant.

By 1972, the eighth year of the Yankee drought, the only consistently bright spot was the moment when relief picher Sparky Lyle came in from the bullpen in a pinstriped car to the strains of "Pomp and Circumstance."

Such show biz touches, which were becoming more and more common throughout baseball, were considered by some purists to be rather crass for the Bronx. But then, what dignity was left for a team mired in the second division?

Dignity? At the end of the 1972 season, during a barbecue in a sportswriter's backyard, two Yankee left-handers, Fritz Peterson and Mike Kekich, agreed to carry out what they called a

Mike Burke, left, president of the Yankees, Lee McPhail, center, general manager of the team, and Ralph Houk, the Yankees manager, all left the team in 1973.

"lifestyle" swap. To the uninitiated: They agreed to trade wives (and children)! This would be radical behavior for most people, even in the 70s, but for baseball players, Yankees at that, it would provide all-time gossip. Peterson was a solid prospect from his rookie season in 1966, when he won 12 games. He won 20 in 1970. He and the ace, Mel Stottlemyre, would be the core of the pitching staff for most of Peterson's eight years in New York.

But Peterson is teamed in history with Kekich, who never won more than 10 games in his four full seasons in New York. Peterson eventually married the former Suzanne Kekich, but the relationship between Kekich and Marilyn Peterson lasted only a few months. Soon after the news broke in spring training, Kekich was shuffled off to Cleveland. Bouton, ever the wry commentator, would say that he could understand men swapping houses, wives and even children, but dogs?

There was a much bigger swap in 1973. The Yankees were sold to a group headed by George Steinbrenner, who said, "I won't be active in the day-to-day operations of the club at all. . . I've got enough headaches with the shipping company."

Right. It was abandon ship for the Yankees. Houk left and replaced Billy Martin as the field manager in Detroit. Lee MacPhail, the general manager, became president of the American League. Mike Burke went off to live a gentleman writer's life in Ireland.

They all must have sensed that Yankee baseball was going to become even more complicated in the Time of the Boss.

Part Four

LIFE WITH STEINBRENNER

(1970s, 80s)

By *Murray Chass*

THE YANKEES made George Steinbrenner famous, but they were not his first brush with New York celebrity. Before he was the owner of a baseball team, Steinbrenner was a Broadway "angel" and had invested in two shows during the 1970s.

"Applause," which opened in 1970, did well at the box office and won a Tony award; "Seesaw," which opened in 1973, did not. The difference, Steinbrenner decided, was the star of each show. Lauren Bacall, he thought, made "Applause" a hit; Michelle Lee, a relative unknown at the time, was unable to work that magic for "Seesaw."

"That always stuck in my bonnet," said Steinbrenner; after he bought the Yankees, he often talked about "putting fannies in the seats." Those fannies must have been much in his mind when, at the close of the 1976 season, Reggie Jackson, one of baseball's biggest stars, became a member of the sport's first class of free agents.

During the season Jackson had said he wanted to stay with the Baltimore Orioles, for whom he had played just one year. But the team had been slow to respond to his agent's overtures, and by season's end, Reggie had changed his mind. He decided he wanted to play for the Los Angeles Dodgers instead.

"I had prayed for the Dodgers to get in it early," Jackson said a quarter of a century later, the details of that November pursuit still vivid in his mind. "The Dodgers were looked at as the number one organization in baseball, like the Steelers and the Cowboys in football. They had their own plane; they trained at Vero Beach. Jackie Robinson was a draw for me."

George Steinbrenner had a different idea. He had decided Jackson would play for the New York Yankees. The Yankees had won the American League pennant in 1976, Steinbrenner's fourth as an owner, but they had been blown away in the World Series by the Cincinnati Reds in a humiliating four-game sweep. What the team needed, Steinbrenner felt, was not only a power hitter, but one with Jackson's extraordinary ability to deliver in big games.

Billy Martin, the Yankees' peppery and opinionated manager, didn't agree. He wanted the Yankees to sign Bert Campaneris, the Oakland Athletics' scrappy shortstop. But Steinbrenner insisted on Jackson, who was also a powerful attraction at the gate.

Steinbrenner had an ally in Gary Walker, Jackson's agent, who also thought the Yankees would make a good fit for his client. But Jackson himself was doubtful. He had once said if he played in New York "they would name a candy bar after me," but for most of his career the Yankees had been a bad team, with little to offer to a star interested in playing for a winner. "The Yankees were not a very good team for a long time," he said. "I related to the Yankee heritage, but I didn't see myself there. The Yankees weren't a real draw for me."

So Steinbrenner went to work as a suitor, pur-

Gabe Paul, center, introducing George Steinbrenner, left, as the new owner of the Yankees in January 1973. Mike Burke, Yankee president, stood behind.

suing Jackson the way a big-time college football coach goes after a star high school quarterback. "We walked around the city," Jackson said. "I met all of his friends. It was an incredible experience. The fans were leaning out of the windows of their cars and buildings. The people at 21. Everybody was so supportive of me coming to New York. George played the tune and I danced."

The Jackson sweepstakes came down to a series of meetings at a Chicago hotel the day before Thanksgiving. The Dodgers weren't there, but the Orioles, the Montreal Expos and the San Diego Padres were. Their representatives met with Jackson, his agent and his lawyer, but when Steinbrenner's turn came, he met one-on-one with Reggie.

After the meeting Steinbrenner left for Culver Military Academy in Indiana, where he planned to have Thanksgiving dinner with his son. But, concerned that one of the other teams might gain

an edge, he returned to Chicago and had breakfast with Jackson on Thanksgiving morning.

In the end, the chase succeeded. "It was like trying to hustle a girl in a bar," Jackson said at the news conference in midtown Manhattan which announced his signing. "Some clubs offered several hundred thousand dollars more, possibly seven figures more, but the reason I'm a Yankee is that George Steinbrenner outhustled everybody else."

George Mitchell Steinbrenner III's passion to win with the Yankees followed his early failure as an owner. He had bought the Cleveland Pipers of the upstart American Basketball League in the early 1960s, but the team failed, costing Steinbrenner at least $250,000, a significant sum at the time.

Steinbrenner bounced back, however, buying his family's ship-building business, Kinsman Marine Transit Company, and acquiring five

Great Lakes ore carriers. He renamed the firm the American Ship Building Company, which had annual revenues of more than $100 million by the time he bought the Yankees in 1972.

The first major-league franchise Steinbrenner had tried to buy was the Cleveland Indians. Only after he failed did he look around for another team. In 1973 Steinbrenner was at Municipal Stadium for an Indians game when he asked Gabe Paul, the Indians' vice president and general manager, if he knew of any other team for sale. At the time, Paul didn't, but not long afterward he told Steinbrenner that the Columbia Broadcasting System was putting the Yankees on the market.

Steinbrenner had always looked forward to seeing the Yankees play in Cleveland. "When the Yankees came to town," he said, "it was like Barnum and Bailey coming to town. I don't mean that they were like a circus, but it was the excitement. They had these gray uniforms, but there was a blue hue to them. I'll never forget them. Watching them warm up was as exciting as watching the game. Being in Cleveland, you couldn't root for them, but you could boo them in awe."

In January 1973, Steinbrenner would finally be able to root. He recruited a group of partners and bought the fabled franchise for $10 million. "I won't be active in the day-to-day operations of the club at all," Steinbrenner said at the Yankee Stadium news conference announcing the deal. "I can't spread myself so thin. I've got enough headaches with my shipping company."

Maybe he believed it at the time, but Steinbrenner was never anything but an active, even intrusive, owner. As John McMullen, a one-time limited partner with the Yankees and later owner of the Houston Astros, wryly remarked several years later, "There's nothing so limited as a limited partner of George Steinbrenner."

IN one of Steinbrenner's first and most ill-advised moves, he slashed the size of the scouting staff. Only later did he understand that scouts are critical to finding promising young players and to uncovering the strengths and weaknesses of opposing teams.

Steinbrenner's attention to detail went beyond baseball. At his first game at Yankee Stadium as the principal owner, he sat in his box seat next to the Yankee dugout as his players stood along the first base line for the national anthem; carefully, he jotted down the uniform numbers of players whose hair was too long and shaggy for his taste and handed the paper to the manager, Ralph Houk. He instructed Houk to tell those players to get haircuts. Back in his office, Houk tossed the paper into the wastebasket and made his first mental note of why he would have to leave the job at the end of the season.

Then there was the trade that the Yankees made for Pat Dobson in June of Steinbrenner's first season. At a Chamber of Commerce lunch in Tampa, Florida, Steinbrenner told a friend, "We've traded Mike Kekich for Pat Dobson." The man later passed the news along to a television sportscaster who congratulated Steinbrenner on the deal in an interview.

"Yes, we've traded Mike Kekich for Pat Dobson," he replied. "It's the shot in the arm we need. We needed a left-handed pitcher and we got one in Dobson." There were only two problems: Dobson was a right-handed pitcher and Kekich was not in the trade.

But that was a minor snafu compared with what happened in Steinbrenner's second year as owner. On the opening day of the 1974 season he was indicted on felony charges for having made illegal corporate contributions to the re-election campaign of President Richard Nixon. Initially Steinbrenner pleaded not guilty to all 14 counts of the indictment, but on August 23 he pleaded guilty to one count each of making illegal campaign contributions and to aiding and abetting obstruction of an investigation, for which he could have received six years in jail. In the end, he was fined $15,000, but avoided prison. (In 1989 he received a presidential pardon from Ronald Reagan.) On November 27, Commissioner Bowie Kuhn suspended Steinbrenner for two years. Although he would remain the principal owner of the Yankees, he was barred from having anything to do with the affairs of the team.

Sixteen days later, with Steinbrenner banished from baseball, Jim "Catfish" Hunter, the star pitcher of the Oakland Athletics, was declared a free agent. A winner of 21 or more games in each of the previous four seasons, the 28-year-old Hunter had landed in his unprecedented position after an arbitrator, Peter Seitz, ruled that Charles O. Finley, owner of the Oakland Athletics, had breached his contract by failing to make a payment on an insurance annuity.

In another year, all players would win the right to free agency, but at the time, no player of Hunter's stature had ever been free to sign with the team of his choice, and 23 of the 24 major-league teams expressed interest in him. For the first time in baseball history, owners and players alike would learn a top player's value on the open market.

Like virtually every other team, the Yankees wanted Hunter, but their owner was out of the chase. Instead, Gabe Paul, once the matchmaker for Steinbrenner's marriage to the Yankees and now the Yankees' president and general manager, was quietly told by his new boss—Kuhn's suspension order notwithstanding—to go to the law office in the small town of Ahoskie, North Carolina, that was representing Hunter and not come back until he could bring the pitcher with him.

The Yankees' chief competition came from the San Diego Padres. Their young general manager, Peter Bavasi, was in Ahoskie offering two McDonald's franchises, courtesy of Ray Kroc, the Padres' owner and the founder of McDonald's. But Catfish was not impressed: "I don't know anything about the hamburger business," he said. "I'm a farmer." The Yankees, too, seemed to be striking out. On December 30, Hunter's lawyers rejected the Yankees' offer, and Paul went home. His retreat, however, was not a surrender. Paul left behind Clyde Kluttz, a former major-league catcher and a Yankee scout. As a scout for the Kansas City Athletics 10 years earlier, Kluttz had signed Hunter out of high school, even though the little toe on Hunter's right foot had been shot off in a hunting accident.

On the morning of December 31, Kluttz did what all the other high-powered baseball executives were unable to do. He ate breakfast with Hunter, then went to the law offices and wrapped up the deal in principle that afternoon. Edward Greenwald, a Cleveland tax attorney and one of Steinbrenner's limited partners, flew in a private plane to pick up Hunter, his four lawyers and Kluttz at a small landing strip in Suffolk, Virginia. En route to New York, Greenwald wrote a 10-page contract in longhand. The lawyers haggled over details after they arrived in New York, but at about 8:30 on New Year's Eve, Hunter signed the contract.

"Clyde never lied to me then, and he never lied to me now," the Yankees' new pitcher said. "If it hadn't been for him, the Yankees would've had a little more trouble signing me." Until Hunter signed on, the highest-paid player in baseball had been Dick Allen, who earned $250,000 with the Chicago White Sox. Now there was a new standard: Hunter's five-year contract was worth $3.35 million. It was the first shot in the free agency wars, and a hint of the explosion in player salaries, and player mobility, that was to change the baseball business in coming years.

Even while under suspension, Steinbrenner was never entirely under wraps. When Ralph Houk resigned as manager after the 1973 season, to retain his dignity and his sanity, he was replaced by Bill Virdon, who had won a division title as manager of the Pittsburgh Pirates in 1972. The unflashy but knowledgeable Virdon managed the Yankees to a creditable second-place finish in 1974, only two games behind the Baltimore Orioles. In 1975 the Yankees were a mere game out of first approaching the All-star Game. But they slipped in the ensuing weeks, and Steinbrenner became nervous.

Billy Martin, who fit Steinbrenner's image of a perfect manager, had become available July 20 when the Texas Rangers fired him, and Steinbrenner privately directed Gabe Paul to find him and hire him, again heedless of Commissioner Kuhn's edict. "Billy Martin is something more than just a baseball manager," Steinbrenner explained later. "In New York, athletics is more than a game. You're in the Big Apple. The game is important, but so is the showmanship involved with the game important. You have to have a blend of capable, proficient players, but you have to have another ingredient in New York and that's color."

Alfred Manuel (Billy) Martin had color all right, often black and blue. He had been a brawler all his life, and he remained one as a manager. "I didn't like to fight, but I didn't have a choice," Martin said, recalling his childhood in West Berkeley, California. "If you walked through the park, a couple kids would come after you. When

you were small, someone was always chasing your ass. I had to fight three kids once because I joined the YMCA. They thought I was getting too ritzy for them."

As a major-league second baseman, he once shattered the jaw of Jim Brewer, an opposing pitcher, in a fight during a game. As a manager, he

Jim "Catfish" Hunter signed to a five-year contract worth $3.35 million in 1974. His contract set a new standard.

Billy Martin had been a brawler all his life. He managed the team 1975–1978, 1979, 1983,1985 and 1988. Here he argues with umpire Jerry Neudecker.

once knocked out Dave Boswell, one of his own pitchers who was fighting another of his players. He punched the traveling secretaries of two teams he managed, a sportswriter in Reno, Nevada, and a marshmallow salesman in Bloomington, Minnesota. He would also suffer a broken arm in a fight with one of his Yankee players, Ed Whitson, one of the few brawls that wound up on the "L" side of his won–lost record.

As a manager, Martin followed a pattern: he would rapidly turn around losing teams, driving them to a division championship. Soon after, he would wear out his welcome with players and management, and get himself fired. He achieved that dubious double with the Minnesota Twins and the Detroit Tigers and almost repeated it with the Rangers.

With that employment record in mind, small wonder that Gabe Paul tried to dissuade Steinbrenner from hiring Martin to manage the Yankees. "Your temperaments aren't compatible," the veteran baseball executive told the owner. "There are going to be problems." But Steinbrenner insisted and Paul tracked down his man to a fishing stream in Colorado. He brought Martin to New York, unveiling him on Old-timers' Day at Shea Stadium, the Yankees' temporary home while Yankee Stadium was undergoing renovation. It was the first of five times that Martin would be introduced as the Yankees' new manager.

THE YANKEES WIN THE PENNANT!
THE YANKEES WIN THE PENNANT!
THE YANKEES WIN THE PENNANT!

Once upon a time, of course, the Yankees *always* won the pennant—there was almost no reason to cheer when it happened. Fifteen times in 18 seasons, from 1947 through 1964, the Yankees won the American League pennant. It was as if they had taken out a copyright on the achievement. But then the copyright expired and the Yankees won no pennants for 11 seasons—their longest drought since they began winning pennants in the Babe Ruth era of the 1920s and 1930s. Steinbrenner realized the team he took over was not a pennant contender; Gabe Paul got the job of doing something about it.

Paul, who had a grandfatherly appearance but a bulldog temperament, would trade anyone if he thought the deal would improve his team. Early in the 1974 season, Paul gave up four popular pitchers—Fritz Peterson, Steve Kline, Fred Beene and Tom Buskey—to his old team, the Indians, in exchange for first baseman Chris Chambliss and pitcher Dick Tidrow. When the trade was announced, many Yankees angrily accused Paul and Steinbrenner of wrecking the team.

"That [trade] was the start of everything," Paul said later, after the Yankees had won three consecutive pennants and two World Series. "It broke up the country club. There was great camaraderie on those losing ball clubs."

On June 15, 1976, even with the team in first place, Paul struck again. In the final hours before the trading deadline, Paul engineered a 10-player trade with the Baltimore Orioles, then purchased Vida Blue's contract from Oakland for $1.5 million. Commissioner Bowie Kuhn, refusing to allow that much money in any transaction, voided the Blue deal. (Kuhn also blocked the purchase

by the Boston Red Sox of Oakland's Joe Rudi and Rollie Fingers for $1 million each.) Yankee catcher Thurman Munson, the American League's Most Valuable Player in 1976, was a player Paul didn't have to acquire. One of the Yankees' few homegrown stars, he was one of only four players on the team's World Series roster who had come up through the Yankees' minor-league system. He also was one of only four who had played for the Yankees before Steinbrenner and his partners bought the team. That was how extensive Paul's overhaul had been.

The new-model Yankees easily won the American League East, but the Kansas City Royals took them to the ninth inning of the fifth and final game of the AL Championship Series. With the game tied 6–6, Chris Chambliss led off the last half of the ninth and swung at Mark Littell's first pitch. The ball landed in the right-field stands, and the long-suffering Yankee fans joyously stormed on the field in such numbers that it resembled an instant mob scene. Much later, after the fans had been dispersed, home plate was nowhere to be found so Chambliss stepped on the spot where it had been. One of the fans had stolen it during the furor on the field.

The Yankees were AL champions for the first time since 1964, but the euphoria didn't last long. The Cincinnati Reds won the first two World Series games at home; then the Big Red Machine, as the team was called, took the next two at Yankee Stadium to wrap up its second successive Series championship. The outcome reduced Billy Martin to tears; it made George Steinbrenner determined not to let it happen again.

"GEORGE? George Steinbrenner? I thought it was you. I just want to meet you and shake your hand. Your team did so much for New York

Thurman Munson was one of the team's few homegrown stars. Here he is tagging out
Dodger Steve Garvey in Game 1 of the 1977 World Series.

this year. I've been waiting more than ten years for this."

"Mr. Steinbrenner, I want to thank you for one marvelous season. I've been a Yankee fan since I was ten years old."

It was two months after the Yankees had won the 1977 World Series, and Steinbrenner was the man of the moment. The Yankees, World Series champions again, their 14-year famine ended. Reggie Jackson had sealed the victory with a spectacular flourish, hitting three home runs against three different Los Angeles Dodgers pitchers in Game 6. Steinbrenner himself would

not have dared to write such a script. But it was the perfect finish to the quest the owner began a year earlier when he designated Jackson as the player to lead the Yankees back to their rightful rank as Number One.

Two developments made it possible for Steinbrenner to execute that plan. Both involved Commissioner Bowie Kuhn.

Under terms of the two-year suspension Kuhn had imposed in 1974, Steinbrenner was not to be restored to active supervision of the Yankees until December 1976. Had he been forced to wait that long, it is likely that Reggie Jackson would

Chris Chambliss is surrounded by fans before he can touch home plate after he hit a ninth-inning, game-winning homer to defeat the Kansas City Royals for the American League Championship on October 14, 1976.

have been signed by another team. But Kuhn had cut short the suspension nine months early, to March 1, allowing Steinbrenner to begin his ardent courtship of Jackson.

Just why Steinbrenner had been reinstated early remains an interesting question. He had applied for reinstatement after one year of suspension, but was turned down. He took the rejection quietly, perhaps convincing Kuhn that the punishment had served its purpose. But Kuhn may also have been influenced by the Yankees' decision the previous July to switch their vote from no to yes in the balloting by owners to

renew Kuhn's contract as commissioner.

Whatever the reason behind Steinbrenner's reinstatement, he would not have had an opportunity to sign Jackson if Kuhn and baseball owners had won their fight over the rights of players to become free agents—the second episode that greatly influenced Steinbrenner's good fortune.

Players had always been bound to their teams by the reserve system. A club "reserved" a player until it chose to trade, sell or release him, and he could go nowhere on his own. Then two pitchers, Andy Messersmith and Dave McNally, challenged the renewal clause in the uniform player's contract, and in December 1975, Peter Seitz, the same arbitrator who had declared Catfish Hunter a free agent a year earlier, ruled that a club could renew a player's contract only once, not perpetually. After that, if the player refused to sign a new contract, he could be free to sign with any team.

Before issuing his decision, Seitz urged the two sides to negotiate a settlement, indicating that he would rule for the players if they did not. But the owners ignored the advice of their labor representative, hoping that they could get Seitz's decision overturned in federal court.

Andy Messersmith speaking at a news conference after meeting with Baseball Commissioner Bowie Kuhn in April 1976. He was challenging baseball's reserve clause.

The owners lost in court, but Marvin Miller, the players' union leader, gave them some relief. Miller understood that the law of supply and demand would destroy the value of free agents if all the players flooded the market every year so Miller agreed that a players would become eligible for free agency only after six years in the major leagues. The new system took effect after the 1976 season, just in time for Jackson to become one of 25 free agents that year.

One night in mid-November, Steinbrenner had dinner with Thurman Munson. Jackson had a reputation for arrogance and Steinbrenner wanted to find out if the other players would accept him. "Go get the big man," Munson told him. "He's the only guy in baseball who can carry a club for a month. And the hell with what you hear. He hustles every minute on the field." Eleven days later, Steinbrenner had his man.

Reggie Jackson did not sneak silently into camp in the spring of 1977. Arriving at the Yankees training camp in Fort Lauderdale, Florida, he declared, "I think Reggie Jackson on your ball club is a part of a show of force. It's a show of power. I help to intimidate the opposition, just because I'm here. That's part of my role." When Jackson made such pronouncements during his nine years with the Athletics, his teammates basically ignored him. They knew that Reggie liked to hear himself talk—especially about himself—and sometimes his remarks even made them laugh.

But his new teammates hadn't had nine years of training, and they often found Jackson infuriating. He would sometimes sit in an aisle seat on the team bus, take out a hefty roll of bills and count them. One day early in the 1977 season, standing outside the team hotel in Kansas City with three reporters, he nonchalantly took out his wallet and began counting $100 bills. As he did so he mentioned that he had just gone shopping with Catfish Hunter and Lou Piniella and that only Piniella had bought anything—some shirts and a $50 pair of shoes. "I wouldn't wear fifty-dollar shoes," Jackson said.

That Reggie was black and made such remarks only made matters worse as far as his new teammates were concerned. "One of the first days in camp, there was a group of guys around the batting rack telling jokes about Kenny Holtzman," Jackson said years later. Holtzman, a pitcher, was Jewish and the jokes were about his religion, not his curveball. "I said to myself, 'I wonder if they know that I'm standing here,'" Jackson said. "I'm a friend of his and I'm black. I wonder what they say about me."

By early in the season, Jackson and Munson had tentatively begun to build a relationship. That the team develop even a fragile friendship was important for the cohesiveness of the team because the catcher was a popular member of the old guard and if he accepted Jackson, so would the rest of the squad. But in May, an article about Jackson in *Sport* magazine reached the

newsstands and any hopes of friendship between the two players shattered, sending pieces flying all over the clubhouse. "I'm the straw that stirs the drink," Jackson said in the article. "Munson thinks he can be the straw that stirs the drink,

Thurman Munson, left, recommended that the team get Reggie Jackson.

but he can only stir it bad."

Jackson's relationship with manager Billy Martin was deteriorating as well. Only a week into the season Martin had benched Jackson for a game because he had told reporters he had a sore elbow. "He didn't know I don't allow players to tell the press about injuries," Martin said.

But when Martin benched Jackson again in May for no apparent reason bigger trouble followed. After hitting a home run a few games later, Jackson took a route from home plate back

New York Yankee manager Billy Martin yells at Reggie Jackson, right, on June 18, 1977, during sixth-inning action in the dugout at Boston. Heated words erupted after Martin took Jackson out of the game.

to the dugout that enabled him to avoid shaking Martin's hand. In doing so, he also snubbed one of his teammates, who had moved to the usual spot to congratulate him.

Matters continued to deteriorate. In Boston on June 18, Martin thought Jackson had loafed going after a hit in right field and yanked him from the game. When Jackson reached the dugout he screamed at Martin, "You never liked me." Martin screamed profanities and Elston Howard, a Yankee coach, had to step between them. All this on national television. Jackson headed up the runway to go to the clubhouse, followed by Martin, who had to be restrained by two other

coaches, Yogi Berra and Dick Howser.

"I ask only one thing of my players—hustle," Martin said later. "It doesn't take any ability to hustle. When they don't hustle, I don't accept that. When a player shows the club up, I show him up."

Jackson exploded. He told the press his side of the story: "It makes me cry the way they treat me on this team. The Yankee pinstripes are Ruth and Gehrig and DiMaggio and Mantle. I'm just a black man to them who doesn't know how to be subservient. I'm a big black man with an IQ of 160 making $700,000 a year, and they treat me like dirt. They've never had anyone like me on

Sparky Lyle being congratulated by Thurman Munson after another save. Lyle was the team's reliever from 1972 to 1978.

their team before." Only Steinbrenner came in for praise. "I love that man," Jackson said. "He treats me like I'm somebody. The rest of them treat me like dirt."

Steinbrenner had watched the dugout scene on television and decided that Martin had to go. But Jackson, of all people, urged the owner to relent. Steinbrenner backed off but told Martin firmly that he would have to change his behavior to keep his job. Martin and Jackson remained civil for the rest of the regular season, but hostilities erupted again during postseason play.

Martin didn't start Jackson in the decisive fifth and final game of the playoff series against Kansas City. The lineup change, he said, was made because two players had told him that Jackson could not hit the Royals' starting pitcher, the left-handed Paul Splittorff. Jackson still managed to contribute to the final 5–3 victory with a pinch-hit single in the eighth inning that narrowed Kansas City's early lead to one run. Jackson was back in the starting lineup when the Yankees began the World Series two days later against the Los Angeles Dodgers. "Splittorff isn't pitching for them," Martin said sarcastically. When Martin's words were relayed to Jackson, he said, "I know what I can do. If he did, we might be a lot better off."

Reggie Jackson hitting his second of his three home runs against the Dodgers in Game 6 of the 1977 World Series.

The next day, it was Martin's turn, "Play your position, do your job and if you can't do your job, shut up," he told reporters in words meant for Jackson. "He's got enough trouble playing right field without second-guessing the manager," adding for good measure that Jackson could "kiss my dago ass."

This time, Jackson restrained himself. In the World Series he singled home a run in the Yankees' victory in Game 3, then belted a double and a home run the next day in another Yankees' victory. But nothing approached his performance in Game 6 at Yankee Stadium.

After he walked and scored in the second inning, Jackson took three swings the rest of the night. On the first he lined Burt Hooton's pitch into the right-field stands for two runs. On the second he smashed Elias Sosa's pitch into the right-field stands for two more runs. On the third he lofted Charlie Hough's knuckleball deep into the unused center-field bleachers for the final run in an 8–4 victory. "I must admit," Steve Garvey, the Dodgers' first baseman, said afterward, "when Reggie hit his third home run and I was sure nobody was looking, I applauded in my glove."

Only Babe Ruth had ever hit three home runs in a World Series game. And not even Ruth ever hit five home runs in a single World Series, as

Jackson did that year. "I don't like the guy," one member of the Yankees said afterward, "but I have to admire what he did. He's a great performer."

JACKSON wasn't the only headliner to have trouble with the irascible Martin. The manager and the owner attacked each other with mutual, open hostility. The two men couldn't even get through spring training in 1977 peacefully.

After the Yankees lost a Saturday night exhibition game to the Mets in St. Petersburg, Florida, Steinbrenner stormed into the Yankees' clubhouse with Gabe Paul. "I ought to get rid of you!" Steinbrenner shouted at Martin. "Why don't you fire me right now!" Martin screamed back, slamming his hand into a tub of ice and splashing water on Steinbrenner and Paul.

In what became the pattern of their relationship, the two men had patched things up by the following morning. They had breakfast together, and the owner apologized for igniting the clubhouse confrontation. "As soon as he apologized," Martin said later, "I knew he'd spend the rest of the season getting my ass." Martin, however, survived the season and was even rewarded with a bonus, or rather three bonuses: $35,000 in cash, a rent-free apartment and a new Diamond Jubilee Mark V Lincoln Continental.

Steinbrenner, elated at winning the World Series in his fifth year as principal owner, also thought their relationship might improve because Gabe Paul was leaving. Paul informed Steinbrenner after the World Series that he was returning to Cleveland and the Indians. Paul had generally been viewed as the buffer between the owner and the manager, but Steinbrenner suggested that "what I was being told" by the president perhaps magnified some of the problems with Martin.

Steinbrenner gracelessly made several other complaints about the man who helped get him to New York and build his team. At 67, he was getting too old for the job, Steinbrenner said, and he had received too much credit for the player moves and the team's success. "He was in baseball for forty years, twenty-five as a general manager, and did he ever win a pennant before?" Steinbrenner asked after Paul had departed. "You think he made all those moves with this team himself? You think all of a sudden he got brilliant?"

To replace Paul, Steinbrenner brought in Al Rosen, a former star third baseman for the Indians, who was working for a hotel/casino company in Las Vegas.

Paul might have been gone, but his final contribution was so important that not even Steinbrenner could diminish it. In the spring of 1977 the Chicago White Sox were prepared to trade Bucky Dent to the Yankees and asked for a package of players that included a young left-handed pitcher named Ron Guidry. Bob Lemon, the White Sox manager, had been the Yankees pitching coach the year before and liked Guidry. Steinbrenner had no problem giving the White Sox Guidry because he had pitched poorly in exhibition games. Paul, though, knew what Lemon knew and said no to the White Sox' request.

A 160-pound Cajun from Lafayette, Louisiana, Guidry didn't look like a power pitcher. And he almost never became one. In 1976 the Yankees sent Guidry to their Syracuse farm team, but he decided to quit instead. He and his wife began the long drive home, but before they had gone far Bonnie Guidry said, "Ron, do you really want to quit? You know you won't be happy not playing ball. Don't do something you'll regret the rest of your life."

Minutes later Guidry made a U-turn and headed toward a career in which he would be a 20-game

Thurman Munson, 15, and Chris Chambliss congratulate Reggie Jackson after his third homer against the Dodgers in Game 6 of the 1977 World Series, a feat unequalled since Babe Ruth's three homers in the 1928 World Series.

winner three times, and in 1978 put on a performance as awesome as any pitcher has ever managed. He won 25 games and lost only 3 for an .893 percentage, the highest ever for a 20-game winner; moreover, he had a 1.74 earned-run average, nine shutouts and 248 strikeouts. In fact, it was with Guidry that Yankee fans began the Stadium tradition of cheering and clapping for a strikeout every time an opposing batter has two strikes against him. In one seven-day period in September that year, Guidry threw successive two-hit shutouts against the Boston Red Sox, who had had led the Yankees by 14 games in July but wound up losing the division championship in a one-game playoff with the Yankees—a game in which Guidry was the winning pitcher.

Babe Ruth crossing home plate after hitting his third home run in Game 4 of the 1928 World Series against the Cardinals. He receives congratulates from Lou Gehrig.

As brilliant as Guidry was in 1978, the Jackson/Martin/Steinbrenner soap opera still frequently managed to steal the headlines. Late in June George Steinbrenner and Billy Martin filmed a television commercial. The script called for the owner and the manager to argue about the merits of a brand of beer. The argument ends when Steinbrenner says, smiling, "Billy, you're fired."

"Oh, no, not again," was Martin's scripted response.

If a beer commercial is considered art, then life nearly imitated it. About the same time he filmed the commercial, Martin nearly got himself fired as a result of a couple of run-ins with Al Rosen and, by extension, Steinbrenner. Rosen, in fact, had made up his mind to fire Martin but instead of doing it directly, he told Martin he was firing Art Fowler, the Yankees' pitching coach. Fowler was Martin's friend and drinking buddy, and Rosen hoped he would resign out of loyalty. "If I can't have the guys around me I want," Martin said, "then you might see something happen." But it didn't happen, not then. It happened a month later.

On the afternoon of July 17 Reggie Jackson had an appointment with Steinbrenner. Jackson had recently been made the team's designated hitter. He saw his new role as a demotion, and he was having difficulty coping with it. Steinbrenner, however, told Jackson that the move was his idea. "I have listened to my baseball people, and they have convinced me that's the move," he said. "I agree that you should be the designated hitter."

An hour and a half later, Jackson walked dejectedly out of Steinbrenner's office on the loge level behind home plate and descended to

Ron Guidry was thinking of quitting the Yankees in 1976. He pitched for the team from 1975–1988. He had three 20-game-winning seasons and in 1978 he was 25-3.

the clubhouse, where he talked to no one. "He just went out for the team picture and didn't say anything to anybody," Martin recalled later.

When that night's game against Kansas City was in the 10th inning tied 5–5, Jackson, without a hit his first four times at bat, went to the plate with a runner at first base and no one out. Dick Howser, the third base coach, flashed bunt, something Jackson hadn't been asked to do all season. The next pitch was high and inside, so Jackson didn't have to bunt. Meanwhile, noticing that the Royals' infielders had moved in, Martin removed the sacrifice sign. But an insulted Jackson bunted

anyway, or tried to. He missed one pitch and fouled off the next two, striking out.

The entire stadium was stunned. Martin was furious. Jackson, anticipating a repeat of the Fenway Park dugout scene, removed his glasses on his return to the dugout and put them on the ledge behind the bench. But Martin kept his distance. Instead he told Gene Michael, the first base coach, to tell Reggie that Roy White would replace him as DH for the rest of the game.

When the game ended after 11 innings, Martin went to his office. He threw a clock radio out the door. He fired an empty beer bottle against a wall. His eyes were red; his body was shaking. As club officials and Martin held a closed-door meeting, Jackson stood at his locker and calmly explained to reporters that he was trying to advance the runner. "I'm not an everyday player. I'm a part-time player. If it was somebody else, there wouldn't be all this crap."

When the door to the manager's office opened, Martin announced that Jackson was suspended for "deliberately disregarding" instructions. "There isn't going to be anybody who defies the manager or management in any way," Martin said, still trembling slightly. "If he comes back again, he does exactly what I say." The loss to the Royals dropped the Yankees 14 games behind the Red Sox, but they won each of the four games Jackson missed during his five-day suspension and were 11 games out when he returned on a Sunday afternoon in Chicago.

Martin was in an unusually jovial frame of mind during Jackson's absence. He smiled and joked and told stories. Then Sunday morning arrived, and his mood abruptly changed. As he sat on the team bus across the street from the hotel, Martin became agitated and impatient. The bus was scheduled to leave at 11:15, and Martin told the traveling secretary there would be no delay.

As he sat in the first passenger seat on the right side facing front, Martin became increasingly edgy. Frank Messer, a Yankees broadcaster with leg and hip problems, started across the street toward the bus and Martin barked to no one in particular, "If Messer's coming, he better walk faster." If Martin was eager to leave to keep Jackson from getting on the bus even seconds late, he need not have worried. Jackson had taken a cab to Comiskey Park. "I'm kind of apprehensive," he explained. "I think it would be better

not to take the bus until I find out what happens."

The clubhouse was filled with reporters. Only Reggie could attract so many, and the newsmen were not disappointed. Standing at his locker, Reggie was deeply emotional. "The magnitude of me," he said "the magnitude of the instance, the magnitude of New York. It's uncomfortable; it's miserable. It's uncomfortable being me; it's uncomfortable being recognized constantly; it's uncomfortable being considered something I'm not, an idol or a monster, something hated or loved."

Jackson sat out that game, too, and the

The Reggie Jackson and Billy Martin soap opera frequently managed to steal the headlines.

Graig Nettles makes one of his trademark diving catches. The Yankee captain played with the team from 1973–1983.

Yankees won again. Now they were 10 games behind the Red Sox. But the winning streak and the standings were not uppermost in Martin's mind. He remained preoccupied with Jackson. Learning from a reporter what Reggie had said, Martin fumed because Jackson refused to admit he had been wrong for defying the manager. After the team bus arrived at O'Hare Airport, Martin stood inside the terminal and berated Jackson. He seemed to be looking for a way to suspend him again.

"I'm saying shut up, Reggie Jackson," Martin said. "We don't need none of your stuff. We're winning without you. We don't need you coming in and making all these comments. If he doesn't shut his mouth, he won't play and I don't care what George says. He can replace me right now if he doesn't like it."

Later, on the way to the gate, Martin resumed his diatribe, calling Jackson a liar and offering examples to prove it. Then he went too far.

Pairing his star and his employer in one contemptuous blast, Martin exploded. "He's a born liar. The two of them deserve each other. One's a born liar; the other's convicted."

When the telephone rang at his home in Tampa at 10:30 that night, Steinbrenner answered and heard a reporter repeat his manager's words. Asked if he had any comment, Steinbrenner could only stammer, "I–I just don't know what to say. I've got to believe that no boss in his right mind would take that." Martin was in the Crown Center Hotel in Kansas City. He had not slept much, and though his agent had spoken with Steinbrenner, Martin had spoken with neither Steinbrenner nor Al Rosen.

By noon, fearing that he was about to be fired, Martin decided to resign. At about 3:30 Monday afternoon he appeared on the balcony level of the hotel lobby, wearing dark glasses and holding his notes in a quivering right hand and a cigar in his left.

Bucky Dent, 20, is greeted by teammates after he hit a three-run homer against the Red Sox to help the team win the division championship on October 2, 1978.

"I don't want to hurt this team's chances for the pennant with this undue publicity," he read. "The team has a shot at the pennant, and I hope they win it. I owe it to my health and my mental well-being to resign. At this time I'm also sorry about these things that were written about George Steinbrenner. He does not deserve them, nor did I say them. I've had my differences with George, but we've been able to resolve them. I would like to thank the Yankee management . . .

the press, the news media, my coaches, my players . . . and most of all . . ." Crying heavily Martin was unable to speak for nearly 10 seconds. Then, almost inaudibly, he added, ". . . the fans." He was quickly led away by a friend, who put his arm around Martin's sagging shoulders.

Sixteen days later Martin had lunch with half a dozen reporters who regularly covered the Yankees. As he picked at a plate of spaghetti, the former manager talked about Jackson.

"I never looked at Reggie as a superstar because he's never shown me he's a superstar," said Martin, tanned and seemingly relaxed but obviously still churning inside. "I look at him as one of twenty-five players. I never put him above Chris Chambliss or Thurman Munson or Willie Randolph or Mickey Rivers or Roy White. There were times I put Fred Stanley above him," Martin added, referring to one of the Yankees' substitute infielders.

The 1978 season would turn out to be one of the most exciting in baseball history. Under Bob Lemon, as stable as Martin had been unstable, the Yankees continued their drive against the Red Sox. They took over first place, then lost the last game of the season and finished in a tie for first with Boston. In a one-game playoff at Fenway Park for the division championship, the Yankees came from behind yet again when Bucky Dent hit an electrifying three-run home run against Mike Torrez in the seventh inning and powered the Yankees to a 5–4 victory.

After that, the Yankees beat the Kansas City Royals for the third consecutive time in the league playoff, lost the first two games of the World Series against the Los Angeles Dodgers and won the next four. They would be the last team

Rich "Goose" Gossage was the Yankees' closer from 1978 to 1983. He also played with the team in 1989.

for 15 years to win two World Series in a row.

But as remarkable as the Yankees' season had been, an event that took place only five days after Martin resigned was perhaps equally remarkable. It was Old-timers' Day at Yankee Stadium and along with the introductions of the team's legendary stars came an announcement from Bob Sheppard, the Yankee's mellifluous-voiced announcer: "Managing the Yankees in the 1980 season, and hopefully for many seasons after that, will be Number 1..." Sheppard did not have to say "Billy Martin." For seven minutes Billy Martin's fans cheered in one of the most incredible scenes ever witnessed in the legendary ballpark.

Steinbrenner, after all, had accepted Martin's apology for his boorish past behavior. "What he said to me," Steinbrenner said, "showed me that he was a man who realized he had made a small mistake, and it was small in the total picture." The owner's forgiveness went only so far, however. Just because he accepted Martin's apology and rehired him didn't mean he trusted him. After the stunning announcement, Steinbrenner rode the elevator to his office. Turning to an aide, the owner said, "Go stay with Billy and make sure he doesn't say anything."

In the end, Martin was once again manager of the Yankees, and then ex-manager, before the date of his scheduled return ever arrived.

In June of 1979, as the Yankees skidded farther from first place than Steinbrenner liked, he fired Bob Lemon and brought back Martin. The Yankees didn't win the pennant that year, and Martin, predictably, got himself in trouble again. Less than a month after the season ended, he punched a 52-year-old marshmallow salesman in a restaurant in Bloomington, Minnesota. Steinbrenner didn't so much object to the punch as he did to Martin's attempt to cover it up. In any

Dick Howser was the new Yankee manager in 1980, the sixth George Steinbrenner had in his seven years as a principal owner.

case, five days later Martin was fired.

It was a fitting conclusion to a season that had turned sour before it was a month old. Rich (Goose) Gossage, whom Steinbrenner had signed as a free agent for the 1978 season, got into a clubhouse fight with Cliff Johnson, a burly designated hitter, and tore a ligament in his right thumb. The injury knocked out Gossage for 12 weeks and the Yankees for the season.

But the real tragedy of the season came in August. Thurman Munson loved to fly airplanes, and when the Yankees had a day off following a

Gene Michael, the former shortstop, was named the team's manager in 1982. He has worked with the team in many capacities.

a marvelous season. Their 103 victories would be the team's highest total between 1963 and 1998, but that wasn't enough for the hard-to-please owner. The Yankees played the Kansas City Royals who, in the playoffs yet again, finally got revenge and swept the league championship series. When Steinbrenner announced yet another managerial change, he said that Howser had received a real estate opportunity that was just too good to pass up. It was news to Howser. As far as he knew, he had been fired.

His successor was Gene (Stick) Michael, the former Yankee shortstop who had served Steinbrenner in any number of capacities, most recently as general manager. The 1981 season was interrupted by a 50-day players strike, and with a month left in the abbreviated season, Michael was replaced by Bob Lemon, who had seen this act before. This time the Yankees reached the World Series, but lost to the Dodgers in six games after winning the first two.

After one of the losses in Los Angeles, Steinbrenner claimed that he had been assaulted by two Dodgers fans in an elevator at the team's hotel, an incident he exploited to fire up his troops. But the players were as cold and empty as Steinbrenner's story. After the series, Steinbrenner issued a bizarre apology to the people of New York for the team's failure—as if the Dodgers had nothing to do with it.

And a famine consumed the land. There would be no more World Series for 14 years, a barren stretch longer than the drought that preceded Steinbrenner's first World Series in 1976.

series in Chicago, Munson went home to Canton, Ohio, to see his family and spend some time flying the $1.4 million Cessna Citation he had just bought. He was practicing takeoffs and landings at the Akron-Canton airport when the plane crashed short of the runway, killing the Yankee catcher.

"He was like a little boy about flying," said Richard Moss, the noted baseball lawyer, who negotiated Munson's last contract. "He talked about getting up in the air alone, being with nature, able to think. And of course, he was able to get home to his family. It was a marvelous thing to him."

When the 1980 season began, Dick Howser was the new manager, Steinbrenner's sixth in seven years as principal owner. Howser, who had been the team's third base coach before leaving to coach on the college level, led the Yankees to

DECLINE AND FALL

Dave Winfield, the Yankee rightfielder, had just one hit in 22 times at bat in the 1981 World Series. According to popular perception, it was that performance that prompted Steinbrenner to label Winfield Mr. May, in contrast to Reggie Jackson's Mr. October nickname. But Steinbrenner invented that unkind label only in September 1985, while Winfield was struggling against the Toronto Blue Jays in a series that was critical to the division race.

In fact, Winfield was usually the productive performer the Yankees expected when they signed him as a free agent in December 1980. He was productive at bat, on the bases and in the outfield. He was big, amazingly athletic, always played hard and was popular with the fans. Perhaps that was why Steinbrenner singled him out for ridicule—an indulgence for which he would pay dearly.

As part of Winfield's free-agent contract, Steinbrenner agreed to make annual contributions to a children's foundation the player had started. But Winfield's agent, Al Frohman, was involved in the foundation and Steinbrenner neither liked him nor trusted him. Frohman, who looked like a character out of "Guys and Dolls," would hang around the Yankee offices and make Steinbrenner uncomfortable. As a result, Steinbrenner did not make the contributions, creating an ongoing, nasty conflict with his biggest star.

Steinbrenner, as a matter of course, liked to

Dave Righetti striking out Wade Boggs of the Red Sox to complete a no-hitter on July 4, 1983.

Dave Winfield was productive at bat, on the bases and in the outfield. He was big, amazingly athletic, played hard and was popular with the fans.

Dave Collins was assured by George Steinbrenner that he would have a spot in the starting lineup in 1982. He played in only 112 games, went to bat fewer than 400 times and was traded after the season.

pick on everyone on the team. He reacted like a fan, saying what was on his mind when he saw a player perform poorly. "We've seen enough of Tucker Ashford," he once said about a young third baseman. "Mike Griffin has fooled us long enough," was his way of dismissing a young pitcher. Jim Beattie, he said, was "scared stiff" pitching against Boston. Ken Clay "spit the bit" when he squandered an early-inning lead against Kansas City.

But Steinbrenner went beyond snide criticisms with Winfield and behaved venomously. For his part, Winfield demonstrated a remarkable ability to sidestep the outbursts and performed beautifully. But while the Jackson-Winfield period (the two stars overlapped in only one year, 1981) produced two World Series championships and four division titles, the Yankees did not return to postseason championship play during Winfield's time after 1981. The plunge into mediocrity was hardly Winfield's fault. As skillfully as Steinbrenner had played the free-agent game

from its creation through the Winfield signing, he lost his touch in the 80s.

Steinbrenner let Jackson leave as a free agent following the 1981 season, blaming the decision in later years on the judgment of Charley Lau, the team's talented hitting coach. Instead of re-signing Jackson, Steinbrenner moved in the opposite direction. He decided that speed was needed, not power, abandoning the hallmark of all previous successful Yankees teams.

Dave Collins epitomized the new Yankee attack. The small, speedy outfielder was a free agent after the 1981 season, and Steinbrenner pursued him even though the Yankees had a full and capable outfield. One November morning Collins and his wife had breakfast with Steinbrenner, who assured him he would have a spot in the starting lineup. As the Collinses went to their hotel room, Kim Collins perceptively asked her husband, "How do you know you can trust him?"

It turned out he couldn't. Playing 60 games in the outfield and 52 at first base, Collins went to bat fewer than 400 times in the 1982 season, which turned out to be his only season with the Yankees. A year after they signed him, they traded

Lou Piniella scoring for the team as the Twins' Ray Smith took the late throw; Graig Nettles looked on. Piniella played for the team from 1974 to 1984.

him. Collins's year in New York was memorable for all his teammates. That season, in which they finished fifth, the Yankees had three managers, three hitting coaches and five pitching coaches. They also had so many players (47) that one day Juan Espino, a young catcher, was there and the next day he wasn't.

"Which one's Espino?" Collins asked one day. You're too late, he was told. Espino was already back in the minors.

If there was another player who epitomized

the wrong-headed decisions of the 80s, it was Ed Whitson, a pitcher. He signed with the Yankees as a free agent for the 1985 season because they offered him the best deal. But neither he nor the Yankees considered what playing in New York might be like for Whitson. The experience almost drove him crazy; he was so ineffective that he became a favorite target for the fans, who rode him so hard that the Yankees stopped using him in home games. The fans didn't limit their assault on Whitson's psyche to the ballpark. One night a car full of rowdy fans followed his car from the Stadium, jeering him menacingly; Whitson said he went through a red light to escape. Another time, he said, he found nails on the driveway at his home in New Jersey.

Clearly, the Yankees weren't going to win any pennants with Whitson or Collins or free-agent pitcher, Andy Hawkins who had only a .500 winning percentage yet was expected to be the anchor of the pitching staff.

What made the Yankees more than mediocre during the 1980s was the bizarre reappearance of Billy Martin, who returned to manage the team three more times in the space of six seasons. Steinbrenner hired him three more times and fired him three more times.

Martin managed the entire 1983 season, the highlight of which may have been the Sunday afternoon game in Milwaukee when his girlfriend (his wife was at home), wearing shorts and a hal-ter top, sat in the club box next to the visitors' dugout and passed notes to Billy with her toes. Steinbrenner fired him at the end of the season—one of his favorite pastimes. He loved to manipulate people like puppets, and he particularly liked to torment Martin. Any time Martin was not managing the Yankees and Steinbrenner remarked that Billy never looked better, it meant that Martin soon would be back as manager. At which point Billy soon stopped looking so good, and would be fired again.

Martin came back 16 games into the season in 1985, after Steinbrenner fired Yogi Berra even though he had promised Berra the full season no matter what happened; he had pulled the same maneuver in 1982, firing Bob Lemon after only 14 games.

The Yankees made a good run at first place in 1985, finishing only two games short, but Billy made a mess of it again. With only two weeks left in the season, he got into two scrapes at the bar in the team's hotel in Baltimore. The second fight was with Ed Whitson, and Martin suffered a broken arm.

Each time Martin came back he seemed less interested in managing. During Term No. 5 in 1988, he was often distracted. He fought more than usual with umpires and he handled the pitching staff badly. He didn't make it to midseason. When Lou Piniella replaced him as manager on June 23 (Piniella had previously followed him in 1986), it marked the end, the real end, to Martin's career.

What would Steinbrenner do now that he didn't have Billy Martin to kick around anymore? Well, he still had Dave Winfield to taunt, and at six feet, six inches tall Winfield made a big target. But finally the owner strayed over the line. A young New Yorker named Howard Spira made Steinbrenner an offer he couldn't refuse. Spira had attached himself to Winfield's agent, Al Frohman, and had acted as a gofer for Frohman and Winfield. From that association, Spira told Steinbrenner, he had learned information that he would be happy to give to Steinbrenner—for a price.

Ed Whitson was ineffective in his starts at Yankee Stadium and became a favorite target for the fans. Here he leaves the mound after allowing five runs on six hits against the Twins in May 1985.

The price turned out to be $40,000, and it led to a nightmare for Steinbrenner worse than the one he faced for making illegal contributions to Richard Nixon's re-election campaign. It turned

Howard Spira made George Steinbrenner an offer he could not refuse. He was found guilty of attempting to blackmail the Yankees' owner with information about Dave Winfield.

out that Spira was an admitted gambler, and Steinbrenner was paying him for dirt on one of his own players. Ever since the fixed World Series of 1919, baseball has been highly allergic to gamblers, so when Commissioner Fay Vincent learned of Steinbrenner's relationship with Spira in March 1990 he opened an investigation. After a hearing Steinbrenner was banished from baseball. In his ruling, Vincent wrote that Steinbrenner had exhibited "a pattern of behavior that borders on the bizarre."

Nothing was more bizarre, however, than the owner's choice of penalties. Vincent initially planned to suspend Steinbrenner for two years and place him on probation for three years, but Steinbrenner asked if there was an alternative penalty. A lifetime ban, Vincent replied. Bingo, Steinbrenner said. His choice of punishment stunned even the commissioner.

Steinbrenner rejected the two-year suspension because he wanted to avoid the label "suspended," thinking it could affect his coveted position as vice president of the United States Olympic Committee. But his decision was nevertheless puzzling, particularly because Steinbrenner indicated that even he might not have understood it. During their discussion of the lifetime ban, Steinbrenner had asked Vincent, "How long does this last?"

In fact, Steinbrenner's lifetime ban did not last a lifetime. An official or a player on the permanently ineligible list is allowed to apply for reinstatement, and Steinbrenner was reinstated in March 1993 after a banishment of approximately two and a half years. It might have been the most beneficial absence the Yankees ever had.

Before stepping down as managing partner, Steinbrenner named Gene Michael as general manager and while Steinbrenner was officially out of the picture (though lurking in the background), Michael laid the groundwork for a minor miracle.

Throughout his 17–year ownership, Steinbrenner had traded away some of the organization's best young players such as Willie McGee, Fred McGriff and Doug Drabek. But Michael had a different view of minor-league prospects; he gave them a chance to make it with the Yankees instead of other major-league teams. As a result, players like Bernie Williams became regulars in the Yankee lineup.

When Steinbrenner returned, he was willing to give Michael's new way a try. Players such as Derek Jeter, Andy Pettitte, Mariano Rivera, Jorge Posada, Ramiro Mendoza and Alfonso Soriano were the beneficiaries. They formed a basis for the Yankees' spectacular success in the 1990s.

George Steinbrenner returned to baseball in 1993 after missing two and a half years. During that period he named Gene Michael general manager. Michael, who believed in the Yankee farm system, laid the groundwork for reshaping the team.

Part Five

THE MODERN YANKEES

───── ❈ ─────

By *Buster Olney*

HIS SUSPENSION was over and George Steinbrenner returned, as subtle as ever. "This team is messed up," he announced shortly to Gene Michael, the general manager who had made the baseball decisions in Steinbrenner's absence. "The players are messed up; everything is messed up. This was in good shape when I left."

"That's why we had the first pick in the '91 draft, right?" Michael responded.

"Don't be a wiseacre," Steinbrenner said, and Michael could smile, knowing he'd applied the needle to his boss in this moment, knowing he was right. The Yankees were a mess before Steinbrenner was suspended in 1990, and as he and Michael quibbled early in the 1993 season the foundation of something good and lasting seemed to be hardening, after a decade of erosion.

Steinbrenner essentially served as his own general manager in the late 1980s, and as Don

Mattingly, Dave Winfield and Willie Randolph aged, the Yankees' roster was packed with former stars who'd become journeymen, players like Steve Sax, Dave LaPoint and Tim Leary. The

Gene Michael speaking at a news conference after he was named general manager and vice president of the Yankees on August 20, 1990. Stump Merrill, Yankee manager, listened.

decline was relentless: second place in 1986, fourth place in 1987, fifth place in 1988 and 1989 and, inevitably, last place in 1990, with the worst record in the American League. Winfield and

Yankee captain Don Mattingly played for the team from 1982 to 1995.

scouts, the general managers, the folks who carried notepads and radar guns to games—his was one of the most respected minds. He had a sense for understanding players, others thought, for recognizing the strengths and weaknesses in their games and their minds, and his evaluations were pure and objective; he cared only about whether or not a player could help a team win, and not about hairstyles or showboating.

Michael had a strong sense of how he wanted to reshape the Yankees. He wanted to emphasize on-base percentage in rebuilding his lineup. If you had more base runners because your hitters produced walks in addition to hits, Michael thought, you would naturally score more runs. He wanted to keep the best of the team's minor-league prospects, rather than trade them; the farm system had been strip-mined during the 1980s, the central reason for the decline.

And Michael wanted to build a roster of players possessing a particular mental toughness—players who could handle New York. Playing for the Yankees, Michael believed, was much different from playing anywhere else. The fans in Yankee Stadium were quick to judge performance, willing to boo anyone, whether it be a star or a rookie just promoted from Class AAA Columbus. The massive media horde probed and demanded, and the thoughts of a disgruntled player could surface like a boil on the back pages of the tabloids. Playing badly was regarded as almost felonious in New York, Michael knew, and he wanted players able to cope with those demands.

A glacial shift in the clubhouse culture of the Yankees was already taking place. Steinbrenner's first championship teams had succeeded despite in-house tension: Reggie vs. Thurman, Billy vs. Reggie, Billy vs. George. But the wild days of the Bronx Zoo were gone and Mattingly had become the leader, his temperament much more like

Randolph were gone, and Mattingly had developed a back problem that dramatically diminished his power and eventually curtailed his career. The best of the free agents, once drawn to New York, now avoided the Yankees, merely using them for negotiating leverage.

Michael was 52 years old when he replaced Pete Peterson as the Yankees' general manager on August 20, 1990, having had a long but mostly undistinguished career in baseball: 10 years as an infielder with four teams, some time as a coach, a year as Steinbrenner's general manager during the 1980 season, a couple of seasons as manager of the Yankees and then the Cubs. Few people outside of the game knew more of him than his nickname, Stick, but among insiders—the

Randolph's than Reggie's. He mostly diffused controversy instead of fostering it, treating teammates respectfully. As the Yankees' star player, Mattingly possessed enormous power, his words and actions potent. With an arched eyebrow or an off-the-record comment to a reporter, Mattingly could've undermined a teammate or new manager Buck Showalter, who took over the team at the outset of the 1992 season.

But Mattingly prepared thoroughly and played hard, always with a professional mien, and as the Yankees injected homegrown minor leaguers and newly acquired players into their roster, they seemed to adopt Mattingly's way for their own. In spring training of 1995, Mattingly worked out with a scatter-armed 20-year-old infielder on a back field of the team's complex in Fort Lauderdale; the rest of the Yankees were playing an exhibition elsewhere. Mattingly and the youngster finished their workout and began walking through an otherwise empty stadium. "Let's run it in," Mattingly told Derek Jeter, "because you never know who's watching," and Mattingly and Jeter sprinted across the field.

There would be mistakes in the reconstruction—foremost, the signing of injury-prone Danny Tartabull before the 1992 season. But Michael added players he judged to be tough-minded, Mike Stanley and Jimmy Key, and he'd taken a chance in trading for an outfielder coming off a bad year. Michael was close friends with Cincinnati manager Lou Piniella and before the 1992 season, Piniella told Michael he intended to turn Reds rightfielder Paul O'Neill into a power hitter. Michael knew Piniella and knew what this meant: Piniella would stand outside of the batting cage and cajole O'Neill, badger him—embarrass him, if necessary.

O'Neill clashed with Piniella, hit only 14 homers and batted just .246 in 1992, and Reds

Paul O'Neill frequently showed explosive displays of frustration.

general manager Jim Bowden called Michael, picking up a thread of previous conversations. How about O'Neill for Roberto Kelly? The deal was made and right away there were questions about whether O'Neill could survive in New York because of his temperament, his explosive displays of frustration. Michael didn't care that O'Neill threw his helmet, or that he sometimes didn't run out ground balls. What he saw in O'Neill was an extraordinary desire to win.

The Yankees won 88 games in 1993, finishing in second place. Steinbrenner was omnipresent again and the same in many respects, bullying and demanding, the phone calls contentious and abrasive. But something had changed in him, as well: Steinbrenner left most of the major deci-

Bernie Williams is another example of the team's strong farm system.

sions in the hands of Michael and the Yankees' other baseball executives, recognizing that something good was happening.

The Yankees' farm system began bearing fruit, talented players like Bernie Williams and Bob Wickman. Michael wasn't sure if they would succeed with the Yankees—Williams, for example, had seemed painfully timid in his first years with the team. Veteran outfielder Mel Hall teased Williams relentlessly about his thick glasses, about his appearance and his shy demeanor, pushing Williams to tears; Michael warned Hall he would be jettisoned if the tormenting continued, and sure enough, Hall was cut loose. But there were questions about Williams's toughness.

Michael considered trade proposals for Williams and for other young players. Montreal offered rightfielder Larry Walker for Williams early in the 1994 season and for a few weeks, Michael came close to agreeing. But Williams hit a few homers and seemed to be improving, and Michael eventually called back the Expos: No, thanks.

The Detroit Tigers intended to trade left-hander David Wells early in the 1995 season and asked the Yankees about some of their prospects, including a slender Class AAA right-hander with a good changeup and a mediocre 88–90 mph fastball that had absolutely no movement—Mariano Rivera. Michael read the reports of a game Rivera pitched for Columbus on June 26, 1995, and was stunned by the radar gun readings, a consistent

95 mph, with flashes of a 96 mph fastball. Michael called the Columbus staff to make sure its radar was operating properly, and he called a scout with another team and confirmed the reading. To this day, neither Michael nor Rivera understand why there had been such a sudden increase in his velocity, but Michael knew immediately after pinning down the radar gun readings that there was no way he was trading Mariano Rivera.

Sterling Hitchcock pitched in 23 games for the Yankees in 1994 and at 23 years old, he was the most developed left-handed pitching prospect in the organization. But another left-hander named Andy Pettitte posted strong numbers in the minor leagues and Michael phoned Tony Cloninger, a pitching coach who worked with Pettitte in Class A. "This guy's got a lot of desire," Cloninger reported to Michael. "He wants to be better than Hitchcock." After the 1995 season, the Yankees negotiated a trade with Seattle and the Mariners wanted either Hitchcock or Pettitte in the trade, and Michael remembered Cloninger's words and recommended that the Yankees keep Pettitte.

The Yankees had the best record in the American League, 70–43, when labor strife ended the 1994 season. Michael will always believe the Yankees would've won the World Series that year. The next season, the Yankees made the playoffs for the first time in 14 years. Williams batted .307, O'Neill hit .300 and the lineup was filled with batters who had the ability to judge the strike zone. The Yankees led the AL in walks in 1994 and 1995, the first time they had done so in back-to-back seasons since 1938–1939.

The Yankees won the first two games of the

Andy Pettitte was a 21-game winner in 1996.

best-of-five Division Series with Seattle but lost the last three games, surrendering a lead in the bottom of the eighth inning of Game 5, and there would be changes. Showalter had managed the Yankees for four consecutive seasons, the longest tenure of any of Steinbrenner's many managers, and became increasingly political in his relationships with the owner, his players and the media; he and Steinbrenner agreed to part ways after the 1995 season. Michael had fought

and argued with Steinbrenner and wore down, unable to let nasty exchanges roll off his back, and he moved into scouting full-time for the Yankees October 23, 1995, 15 days after the Mariners' Ken Griffey Jr. slid across home plate with the decisive run of the Division Series.

Steinbrenner solicits input from a range of sources, former scouts or players or agents or friends, sometimes frustrating club officials hired to provide advice. He did not have a stand-out candidate to replace Showalter in the fall of 1995, but Arthur Richman, a media relations executive, pestered him to hire Joe Torre—not exactly the dynamic hire Steinbrenner sought. Torre had managed the Mets, Braves and Cardinals after a long playing career, without ever appearing in the World Series. He was 55 years old, and Steinbrenner already had passed him over as a general manager candidate, hiring Bob Watson instead.

"He'd be perfect for New York," Richman insisted, citing Torre's Brooklyn roots. Steinbrenner decided to hire Torre, and for years afterward the owner taunted reporters about one initial response to Torre's employment, which came in the form of a back page tabloid headline: CLUELESS JOE.

Torre bore a reputation for being a players' manager, not always a compliment; at the end of his tenure with the Cardinals, some St. Louis

Joe Torre was not the dynamic hire George Steinbrenner sought. Since Torre was hired he has won four World Championships.

executives felt he didn't demand enough of his players. It was apparent early in his tenure with the Yankees, however, that his personality would suit his team extraordinarily. Showalter was tense and controlling and wore on some of his veterans; in contrast, Torre sat stoically in the Yankees' dugout, muttering to coaches Don Zimmer and Mel Stottlemyre, his face mostly remaining expressionless through good innings and bad innings, through losing streaks and winning streaks. Managing in the hot cauldron that is the Yankees' world, Torre always seemed to diffuse controversy, rather than stoke it, thereby reducing the pressure on his players—and, over time, Torre came to view this as perhaps the most important aspect of his job.

Tino Martinez was the regular first baseman for the team from 1996 to 2001.

The players came to appreciate the respect Torre showed for them, something they felt every time he came to them to deal directly with an issue before he spoke to the media, and they returned the respect by generally accepting his decisions without open complaint. He would bench veteran position players like Tino Martinez, Cecil Fielder, Darryl Strawberry, Tim Raines, Chuck Knoblauch and Paul O'Neill during his tenure as Yankees manager, bypass pitchers like Roger Clemens, David Cone and Andy Pettitte—and he still avoided serious backlash, because of his relationship with his team.

He spoke with players about coping with slumps and had credibility because of his extensive playing career. He spoke about the frustrations of losing, and could draw from experience—when Torre joined the Yankees, he had never appeared in a World Series game as a player or manager. That would be the lingering question about Steinbrenner's new manager as the Yankees began play in September of 1996, in first place but struggling to hold off the Baltimore Orioles. The Yankees' lead was cut to single digits and Torre held a team meeting and announced emphatically to his players that they were going to win the division.

Joe Girardi played with the team from 1996 to 1999.

turn crimson by the third inning, sweat trickling down his face. He refused to give into hitters, sometimes walking two or three batters in an inning instead of conceding a meaty fastball over the plate. On those days when he didn't have his best stuff—a slider that dove away from right-handed hitters, a splitter that faded under the swings of left-handed hitters—he would make an adjustment in his arm angle or seemingly invent a pitch and fight his way out of jams.

Cone came back to pitch in the last weeks of the 1996 season, and as Torre had asserted, the Yankees held off the Orioles to win the AL East, their first division title in 15 years. They would face the Orioles again in the championship series, and in Game 1, their rookie shortstop responded under pressure, in the first of many significant postseason moments for him.

Derek Jeter was 21 in spring training of 1996 and there was much sentiment within the organization that he was too raw and too erratic defensively to play in the majors. But Torre loved his attitude—Jeter radiated confidence—and he and others concluded that, over the course of the season, he would settle defensively and contribute offensively, with his speed and his inside-out swing. By season's end, Torre was convinced Jeter was going to be a major star; he accepted responsibility, acknowledged mistakes and worked to correct them and seemed to crave pressure. Others in baseball who'd known Jeter since he played at Kalamazoo Central High in Michigan saw the same thing. Hal Newhouser, a former major-league star who scouted for Houston in 1992, begged the Astros to draft Jeter that year with the first selection in the draft. This kid will be the shortstop for a team that plays in many World Series, Newhouser reported, raving about Jeter's makeup. The Astros, needing immediate help and unsure whether Jeter would

Some of the leaders from Showalter's teams had departed—Mattingly was retired and Stanley had gone to Boston, replaced by the likes of Tino Martinez and Joe Girardi. But the clubhouse dynamic remained the same, the players sharing a mutual respect. Cone had been acquired for the stretch drive in 1995, became a free agent and nearly signed with the Baltimore Orioles for the 1996 season. He returned to the Yankees, however, and despite missing much of that year with an aneurysm, his voice was always one of the most prominent in team meetings. Torre trusted him immensely, sometimes recruiting him to help with internal issues, and he appreciated Cone's competitiveness. When he pitched, Cone's face would

David Cone came back from an aneurysm to pitch in the last weeks of the 1996 season.

decide to attend college, bypassed Jeter and selected Phil Nevin instead. Newhouser, 71 years old, resigned his job after a lifetime in baseball, retiring in frustration.

The Yankees trailed the Orioles by a run in the bottom of the eighth inning of Game 1, and Jeter smashed a long drive to right field. As Oriole rightfielder Tony Tarasco set himself against the wall and reached for the ball, a glove appeared above him, and Jeter's fly disappeared into the stands. Rich Garcia, the umpire assigned to right field, twirled his index finger to indicate a home run, and soon found himself surrounded by infuriated Orioles. As television replay clearly showed, 12-year-old Jeffrey Maier had knocked the ball over the wall as he attempted to catch it—Garcia admitted after the game that he had blown the call—but Jeter's home run stood, tying the game. Years later, when Oriole third baseman Cal Ripken spoke before his final game in Yankee Stadium, he mentioned Jeffrey Maier,

whose name will forever remain notorious in Baltimore.

The Yankees won that game in extra innings and defeated the Orioles in five games in the series. The excitement over the pennant quickly dissipated, however, when the Atlanta Braves won the first two games of the World Series in Yankee Stadium. Steinbrenner spoke to Torre after Game 2 and mentioned, fearfully, that he was worried that the team would be swept and embarrassed. Torre assured Steinbrenner that the Yankees would be fine, feeling as if his team was destined to win.

Torre had aligned his rotation so that the veteran Cone would pitch Game 3 on the road, and Cone held the Braves to a run over six innings and turned over a lead to Rivera and closer John Wetteland. The momentum from the Game 3 victory was quickly lost early in Game 4, however, when Kenny Rogers imploded and the Yankees fell behind, 6–0. The Yankees scored three runs

Derek Jeter radiated confidence in his rookie season in 1996, and manager
Joe Torre was convinced he was going to be a major star.

in the sixth inning, cutting Atlanta's lead in half, and Braves manager Bobby Cox was forced to summon relievers from his exhausted bullpen. Two runners reached base in the eighth inning and hard-throwing Braves closer Mark Wohlers faced Jim Leyritz, who fought off Wohlers's fastball, fouling off pitches, spinning the bat in his right hand after each swing. Wohlers, looking for a way to finish off Leyritz, decided to try a 2-2 slider, and spun the pitch high in the strike zone. Leyritz swung, and if there was a precise moment when the Yankees' current dynasty began, this was probably it: Leyritz's drive crash-landed over the left-field fence, tying the game, and the Yankees won in extra innings, the lead run crossing the plate when Wade Boggs drew a bases-loaded walk.

Pettitte pitched the next day, in Game 5, ferry-

Jim Leyritz watching his 3-run homer in Game 4 against
the Braves in Atlanta in 1996.

ing a 1–0 lead into the ninth inning. With two runners on and two outs in the bottom of the ninth,
Wetteland fired fastball after fastball at Atlanta
pinchhitter Luis Polonia, who kept fouling off
pitches, his swings getting better and better.
During the at-bat, outfield coach Jose Cardenal
stood in the Yankees' dugout and motioned to
O'Neill in right field, prodding O'Neill to move a
little more to his right, toward the gap. O'Neill,
hampered by a bad hamstring, shifted as he was
instructed to do. Wetteland threw another fastball, Polonia ripped a line drive toward right-
center field and O'Neill, sprinting on his gimpy
leg, striding, stretching and reaching for the ball,
made the catch to end the game. The Yankees
had swept the Braves in Atlanta and two days
later, Atlanta's Mark Lemke lifted a pop fly to the
third-base side in the ninth inning, and when

Reliever John Wetteland, with arm raised, celebrates with teammates after
their World Series victory against the Braves in 1996.

Charlie Hayes squeezed the ball in foul territory, Yankee Stadium became a house of bedlam, a mob of players surrounding Wetteland on the mound. As many of the players circled the field to salute fans who screamed for them, Boggs jumped onto a police horse, waving ecstatically as he rode behind one of New York's finest. The Yankees were champions again—and would be again, again and again.

But they would lose to Cleveland in the 1997 Division Series and the defeat gnawed at the Yankees in the off-season. They had played well in the last month of that season, went into the playoffs as the defending champions and, as Bernie Williams recalled, they fully expected to prevail again. The Yankees were on the verge of wrapping up the series in Game 4 when Indian catcher Sandy Alomar smashed a game-tying

Wade Boggs rides a police horse as he celebrates with fans after the team defeated the Braves for the World Championship at Yankee Stadium in 1996.

opposite-field home run in the bottom of the eighth off Mariano Rivera, who was in his first postseason as the Yankees' closer. The Indians won Game 4 in the bottom of the ninth, and held off the Yankees in Game 5. When Williams flied out to end the Yankees' season, disbelief filled his face. O'Neill returned to his Ohio home and found it almost impossible to watch any more of the playoffs and the World Series; he just couldn't fathom the notion that the Yankees weren't participating.

Torre wrote to Rivera in the off-season, one note among many notes he penned to his players, and through his words, he aimed to help Rivera get past the Alomar home run, to move on—something many closers in baseball history have been unable to do after surrendering a crucial hit. What Torre would not know until the next season, however, was that Rivera had quickly found peace of mind. Rivera spent some time thinking about the home run, mulled over the

location and pitch selection, and this is what he decided: Alomar's home run was freak luck made possible only because of Rivera's dominance, not in spite of it. Rivera's fastball generated the power needed for an opposite-field home run, he thought. Alomar had happened to intercept the pitch at precisely the right moment. Even in a moment of devastating defeat, Rivera—his confidence as resolute as a 10-foot bank of steel—had reached the conclusion that he had a great and nearly unhittable fastball. Nearly 1,500 days would pass before he again contributed to a Yankee loss in the postseason.

Steinbrenner spurred his front office into more tangible changes. The Yankees of 1997 had been bogged down by internal problems: the contract dispute with Cecil Fielder, the fight for playing time between Wade Boggs and Charlie Hayes, the arrests of Dwight Gooden and Mark Whiten, the untenable plight of pitcher Kenny Rogers, who had never adapted to New York. All of those

BAT BALL STRIKE OUT INN
0 0 0 9

David Wells celebrating his perfect game on May 18, 1998.

players were jettisoned in the off-season. The Yankees dumped Rogers on the Oakland Athletics, receiving little-known third baseman Scott Brosius in return; Brosius could be a solid utilityman, Yankees' officials thought at the time, if it turned out he couldn't hit enough to be the everyday third baseman. The Yankees also pressed to acquire a lead-off hitter, and less than two weeks before the start of spring training in 1998, they dealt for Chuck Knoblauch, a Gold Glove second baseman considered the best lead-off man in the game.

But it was Brian Cashman, and not Bob Watson, who concluded that trade. Watson, feel-

ing run down after little more than two years of dealing with Steinbrenner, resigned and recommended that the 30-year-old Cashman take his place.

The Yankees looked invincible in spring training, the lineup extraordinarily deep, Knoblauch and Jeter at the top, O'Neill in the third slot and Williams the cleanup hitter. The Yankees lost their first three games and four of their first five, however, and after some of the position players became enraged when Pettitte did not retaliate for a hit batsman in Seattle, Joe Girardi and David Cone and other veterans called a team meeting. They were too good to be playing so poorly, it was agreed, and what none of them knew at the time was that the Yankees would win 36 of their next 43 games and begin to establish themselves as one of the greatest teams in baseball history.

The sentinel moment over those months occurred on May 17. The Yankees played the Minnesota Twins on a Sunday afternoon in Yankee Stadium, and their starting pitcher was hung over. David Wells hated working in day games, because he was a creature of the night and he sometimes needed the afternoon hours to eradicate the dull ache rooted in his taste for liquor. But Wells felt unusually strong early against the Twins that day, pumping his fastball, spinning his curve, his command impeccable. No one ever doubted his talent, only his dedication, and despite being left-handed and blessed with extraordinary endurance, Wells bounced from the Toronto Blue Jays to the Detroit Tigers to the Cincinnati Reds to the Baltimore Orioles to the Yankees, angering Torre repeatedly in 1997, the first season he was with the team. Wells once took the mound in a cap worn by Babe Ruth, until Torre ordered him to remove it, and in another game, he was ejected early at a time when the team was operating with an exhausted bullpen.

He and Torre had another blowup early in the 1998 season in Texas, when after Wells botched an eight-run lead Torre openly questioned the conditioning of the burly pitcher. The two men and pitching coach Mel Stottlemyre met in private several days later and discussed their issues. This satisfied Wells and seemed to calm him; just days later, he pitched against the Twins, on that Sunday afternoon, his stuff all but unhittable.

Orlando "El Duque" Hernandez demonstrates his unusual delivery as he pitches for the team.

Wells retired the first 18 batters and from inning to inning, teammates gave him more and more room on the bench, not wanting to have any contact with the pitcher, lest they jinx his perfect game. The crowd was roaring at every out, but nobody was saying anything in the dugout and Wells, his hands beginning to shake

Scott Brosius celebrates the team's World Series victory over the Padres in 1998. He was named the series' Most Valuable Player.

fect game against the Montreal Expos. Stranger than fiction, this.)

The Yankees clinched a playoff spot before August ended in 1998, wrapped up their division in early September and finished the regular season with a record of 114–48, shattering the American League record of 111 wins set by the 1954 Cleveland Indians (Seattle broke the Yankees' record in 2001, winning 116 games). The second game of an August 4 doubleheader in Oakland symbolized the Yankees' dominance in 1998. The Bombers had obliterated the Athletics the day before, 14–1, and routed Oakland in the first game of the doubleheader, 10–4. But in the second game, former Yankee Kenny Rogers shut them down in the first eight innings. Oakland led, 5–1, going into the last inning, but Tino Martinez and Tim Raines singled to open the ninth and right away, a sense of inevitability hung over the game; the Yankees trailed by four runs but a small band of their fans cheered loudly behind their dugout. They were so overpowering, so deep, and played with such incredible, lasting intensity. A comeback seemed predestined.

Third baseman Mike Blowers bobbled a grounder to load the bases and Darryl Strawberry stepped out of the dugout to pinch-hit for Joe Girardi. If you watched the Yankees on that night and throughout that season, it felt like an absolute certainty that Strawberry was going to hit a home run. Billy Taylor, the Athletics' reliever, threw a fastball, and Strawberry buggy-whipped his bat through the strike zone. Not only did he launch the game-tying grand slam, but he also blasted the ball to straightaway center field. His teammates jumped and danced in front of the visitors' dugout, and the Yankees went on to score five more runs that inning, winning 10–5. The incredible became predictable that year.

But the Yankees were pushed in the American

from nervousness, was desperate to talk to somebody. Finally, Cone broke the tension during the eighth inning. "I think it's time to break out the knuckleball," he said, and Wells laughed.

Wells retired the first two batters in the top of the ninth inning, and when Pat Meares lifted a fly-ball to right field, Wells bounced and grinned until O'Neill caught the ball, and then Wells pumped his fist downward. It was the first perfect game at Yankee Stadium since Don Larsen's Game 5 outing in the 1956 World Series—incredibly, Larsen, like Wells, was a graduate of Point Loma High School in San Diego. (There would be a postscript the next summer, on July 18, 1999. Larsen appeared at Yankee Stadium to throw out the first ball to Yogi Berra and watched from Steinbrenner's private box as Cone pitched a per-

League Championship Series by the same team that had devastated them in 1997. The Cleveland Indians won Game 2 of the best-of-seven series in Yankee Stadium, and then took Game 3. The Yankees desperately needed Game 4 to tie the series, and snow was forecast for Jacobs Field that night. Torre had no idea how his starting pitcher would cope with the cold, or the inherent pressure in the game. Orlando Hernandez had pitched in important international games in his homeland of Cuba, but he'd been in the majors only four months, in the U.S. only seven months. Hernandez slipped out of Cuba the previous December aboard a boat and signed with the Yankees in March, despite lingering questions about his age. "If he signs with us, then he's 28," said Cashman, "and if he signs with another team, he has wooden teeth, as far as I'm concerned."

The first scouts who saw Hernandez fretted about whether he had enough velocity on his fastball, and thought his unusual delivery—he drew his left knee close to his cheek, hiding the ball behind his right hip—might have to be restructured. Hernandez threw well in his debut, in June, and the Yankee Stadium crowd responded enthusiastically to him. But Torre still preferred to keep Ramiro Mendoza in the rotation—Mendoza had earned the spot, Torre felt. Steinbrenner stepped in and ordered El Duque to remain in the rotation, however, and in October, the Yankees' record-breaking season hinged on Hernandez.

Torre went to the restaurant in the team hotel on the day of Game 4 and saw Hernandez grinning and laughing while serving food to friends, and was greatly relieved; Hernandez did not seem at all nervous. Nor did Hernandez appear anxious during the sixth inning that night, when massive Cleveland slugger Jim Thome stood at the plate as the potential tying run. The count was 3 balls and 2 strikes and Hernandez threw a changeup to Thome, using a grip he had learned only months before; Thome swung and missed. The Yankees won that game, and went on to defeat the Indians in the series and sweep San Diego in the World Series, the whole postseason turning on what was the first of a dozen extraordinary October performances by Hernandez.

BROSIUS won the Most Valuable Player Award for the 1998 World Series, but was absent from most of the postgame clubhouse celebration and declined the standard invitation from Disney. Instead, Brosius ducked into the room where family and friends gathered, to see his father, Maury, who was dying, suffering from an aggressive form of cancer.

As the Yankees became an irresistible force on the field, they were touched repeatedly by the tragedies and trials of the human condition. Torre lost one brother during the 1996 season, Rocco, to a heart attack, and Frank Torre, the manager's other brother, underwent a successful heart transplant in the midst of the World Series that year—a numbing sequence of events that felt surreal, Joe Torre would say afterward. Less than three years later, in March of 1999, the manager was diagnosed with prostate cancer, and he summoned some of his veteran players into his office to inform them of his condition. Torre initially thought about retiring; the last thing in the world he cared about in the first days after the diagnosis, he would say, was baseball. Torre left the team and his old friend Zimmer became the interim manager, but two months after his surgery, Torre rejoined the Yankees as they began a series in Boston. He walked the lineup card to home plate and was touched when fans in Fenway Park stood and clapped for him.

The team celebrates their World Series
victory over the Braves in 1999.

"It's seems like everyone is getting cancer," Jeter said incredulously at the time, fear in his words. Just before the playoffs began in 1998, Strawberry finally sought treatment for the pain he had felt in his abdomen for two months and underwent testing, and was diagnosed with colon cancer. Torre told his players of Strawberry's condition in a team meeting and players emerged silently from the clubhouse, some—like Cone, Strawberry's long-time teammate—overcome by tears. Strawberry became a source of motivation for them in that postseason, and they visited him in the hospital, phoned him after big wins, hugged him at the World Series parade. But Strawberry, addicted to alcohol and cocaine since his days with the Mets and constantly fighting those chemical dependencies, was arrested the following spring for possession of cocaine

Derek Jeter celebrates his team's World Series victory over the
Braves in 1999 by spraying fans with champagne.

and solicitation of prostitution, in the midst of his chemotherapy. Although Strawberry returned to play in the 1999 World Series—somehow, through all his troubles, he managed to retain that beautiful, powerful swing—it was clear that he had begun to lose his grip on sobriety. He was suspended from baseball after failing a drug test in February of 2000, violated the terms of his probation and was imprisoned by the state of Florida. Teammates rarely called anymore, unsure of what to say.

As Brosius coped with the deteriorating condition of his father in 1999, torn because his work kept him far away from their Oregon homes, Paul O'Neill's father, Charles O'Neill, fell ill. The off-field concerns hung over the Yankees throughout that year. Brosius left the team for a week at one point, with the blessing of Torre and Cashman, to spend time with his father—to say things that needed to be said between father and son, Brosius explained afterward. Maury Brosius

passed away in September and Brosius left the Yankees again, tending to family matters. Brosius said later he would always be grateful for the way Torre and the Yankees handled his situation; otherwise, Brosius said, he would've forever resented baseball.

Luis Sojo's father passed away just before the 1999 World Series, and as Sojo took his father's body back to Venezuela, the Yankees played the first two games of the World Series with 24 available players, rather than 25. Then, the night before Game 4, Charles O'Neill passed away. Torre spoke to his distraught rightfielder early in the afternoon and told him that, of course, nobody expected him to play.

But O'Neill asked to be in the lineup, and he was on the field when Chad Curtis caught the last flyball to end the game and the Series. O'Neill jogged in slowly from his position and was among the last Yankees to approach the joyous celebration in the infield. Torre hugged O'Neill

Chuck Knoblauch had a history of throwing problems.

and whispered in his ear that his father was watching and was proud, and O'Neill, covering his eyes, ran off the field, finding privacy in a back room at Yankee Stadium. Clemens, who pitched and won Game 4, joined O'Neill. He had lost his own father to a heart attack when he was a boy, and Clemens talked about how wonderful it had been—a gift—that Charles O'Neill had seen Paul play in the majors, to share in that experience. The following spring, Stottlemyre—with whom Clemens had become very close—

was diagnosed with a form of blood cancer, and he would miss most the last two months of the season as he received treatment. Early in the 2001 season, Bernie Williams lost his father, as well.

Ray Knoblauch had been the central figure in the life of his son, coaching Chuck through Little League and into high school baseball, teaching him fundamentals that became almost instinctive for the boy. By 1998 Ray Knoblauch was beset with Alzheimer's. Chuck Knoblauch never speculated openly on what impact his father's illness had on him; some of his teammates were sure, however, that the inexplicable and extraordinary throwing problem that began plaguing Knoblauch in his first season with the Yankees was somehow tied to his father's situation. Ray Knoblauch had always been there to diagnose problems and offer suggestions, and as Chuck Knoblauch began to throw the ball tentatively in spring training of 1998—flipping the ball while running toward first base, with his arm cocked uncomfortably at a right angle—there was no place for the son to turn.

Knoblauch's throwing problems were dormant in the second half of the 1998 season, appeared again in 1999 and festered to the point that Torre began replacing him late in games. Then, in 2000, the jitters manifested themselves fully, Knoblauch sometimes missing his target by 20 feet or more. Torre began using him as a designated hitter, and never put him in the field during the playoffs or World Series that fall, benching him in the games played at Shea Stadium. Knoblauch spoke with psychiatrists and practiced hundreds of hours in an attempt to conquer his problem before the 2001 season, to no avail. Shortly before the 2001 season began, Torre finally decided to shift Knoblauch to the outfield. Chuck Knoblauch came to the Yankees as a borderline Hall of Fame candidate and was an integral member of three championship teams, but he left the team in the 2001–2002 off-season with his career essentially in ruins.

Their success never frightened the Yankees away from considering major changes from year to year. Williams became a free agent after the 1998 season and the Yankees prepared to let him go, some in the organization believing he was not worth the seven-year deal his agent sought. Williams had developed from that timid young player into an All-star, averaging 100 RBI per season from 1996 to 1998, but he missed about 20 to 30 games a year with injuries and was not a consistently dominant offensive force. For the kind of money Williams wanted, the Yankees wanted a more dynamic hitter—and they set their sights on another high profile free agent, Albert Belle.

Torre played a round of golf with Belle, negotiations intensified, the Yankees offered Belle a four-year, $52 million deal; Williams, it appeared, was going to sign with the Boston Red Sox. Fifteen minutes after Belle agreed to the deal, however, his agent informed Cashman that the slugger had changed his mind. Steinbrenner phoned Williams's agent and during a 20-minute conversation, Steinbrenner increased his offer by nearly 50 percent, from $60 million to $87.5 million over seven years. Within three years, Belle's career was over and Williams was still an integral member of the team, an extraordinarily fortunate turn of events for the Yankees.

They were lucky the following summer, as well, in bypassing a deal. Andy Pettitte had been in steady decline since 1996 and by the middle of 1999, he was confused and frustrated and largely ineffective, allowing more than five runs per game. Steinbrenner ordered Cashman to solicit offers for the left-hander and the day before the trade deadline, Philadelphia forwarded an acceptable proposal of three young players. But Cashman, Torre and Stottlemyre vehemently argued against trading Pettitte, and Steinbrenner relented, with a caveat: If this turns out to be a bad move, you guys will be held responsible. Pettitte rebounded, pitched well in the postseason and reestablished himself as one of the league's best left-handers.

Clemens played a role in Pettitte's comeback, mentoring him, convincing Pettitte to intensify his workouts. Pettitte was important for

Mike Piazza breaking his bat on a foul ball in the first inning as he faced Roger Clemens in the 2000 World Series.

Clemens, as well, helping the fellow Texan become acclimated after the Yankees traded Wells, reliever Graeme Lloyd and infielder Homer Bush for Clemens—a trade hugely unpopular among Yankee fans who loved Wells and had always despised Clemens, formerly the ace of the hated Red Sox.

On one of Clemens's first days with the Yankees he threw live batting practice against some of his new teammates, hitters who had been plunked by Clemens in the past. Knoblauch and Jeter walked into the batting cage wearing a complete wardrobe of protective gear, and Clemens grinned broadly. Past tensions were soon forgotten, but Torre thought it took Clemens months to get comfortable—Torre wondered, also, if Clemens was bothered by some leg ailments— and Clemens pitched erratically in his first year

Roger Clemens throwing Mike Piazza's broken bat in
the direction of the catcher.

with the team, fans at Yankee Stadium occasionally booing him. A power pitcher throughout his
career, Clemens seemed to be throwing an unusually high ratio of breaking pitches early in the ball-
strike count, Stottlemyre thought. Pettitte sat in
the dugout and watched his idol and sometimes
wondered: Where's the fastball?

Midway through the 2000 season, however,
Clemens regained his dominance, throwing 96–97

mph consistently. From July 2, 2000, to September
25, 2001, Clemens won 29 of 32 regular-season
outings, and became one of the core members of
the Yankees, a leader deeply respected by teammates for his work ethic and competitiveness.
Before games Clemens would shave his body, as
swimmers do, and he would be covered with a
heat balm that had a Ben-Gay–like scent that filled
the nostrils of teammates in the infield. Clemens

then shoved a blue mouth guard over his lower jaw, straddled the mound in a gunfighter's stance and peered in at the catcher, his black glove and his cap shielding his entire face from the hitter except for his eyes. Clemens loved this part of the game: the competition, the intimidation.

Clemens's reputation for knocking down hitters had long been established before he pitched against the Mets in an interleague game on July 8, 2000. Mike Piazza, the Mets' catcher, had wrecked Clemens in their previous meetings, col-

Luis Sojo, with his unorthodox batting stance, had great ability to make contact with the ball.

lecting 7 hits in 12 at-bats. Clemens wanted to change the tenor of their matchups, and acknowledged he wanted to pitch Piazza inside. But Clemens beaned Piazza with a 96 mph fastball, and as Piazza fell to the ground he stared upward, blinking blankly. Clemens immediately crouched on the mound after Piazza went down, appearing upset, and he attempted to phone Piazza during the game to apologize. Piazza wouldn't accept the call; in the instant that it required for Clemens's fastball to bounce against Piazza's helmeted head, the nature of the rivalry between the Yankees and Mets changed. The incident would serve as the backdrop for the first Subway Series in 44 years.

The Yankees barely survived the first round of the playoffs, winning the fifth and deciding game of the Division Series against Oakland with exceptional relief from Mike Stanton, Jeff Nelson, Orlando Hernandez and Mariano Rivera. Clemens threw one of the greatest games in postseason history against the Seattle Mariners in the AL Championship Series, allowing one hit and striking out 15, hitting 99 mph on the radar gun in the ninth inning. The Yankees finished off Seattle the night after the Mets clinched the National League title, and the dreams and fears of baseball fans in the city were realized.

The Mets had played better baseball than the Yankees had in the month leading to the World Series, and in Game 1, they led by a run going into the bottom of the ninth inning. But they probably should've led by more. The Mets' Timo Perez had been thrown out at home plate in the

The Yankees celebrate their 26th World Championship
as they defeated the Mets in 2000.

sixth inning, because he'd assumed, wrongly, that Todd Zeile's line drive to left was going to clear the fence and began to trot nonchalantly home. Armando Benitez entered the game to pitch the bottom of the ninth, retiring Jorge Posada; the Mets were two outs away from winning the first game of the series in Yankee Stadium.

O'Neill came to bat, still caught in a slump that began in early September, still nagged by injury, dropped to seventh in Torre's lineup. The Athletics and the Mariners had enjoyed great success against O'Neill by jamming him with fastballs, seizing on what appeared to be his diminished bat speed. Benitez fired 96–98 mph fastballs at O'Neill, but outside, and O'Neill bare-

ly managed to fight them off, fouling pitch after pitch into the stands on the third-base side, his swing late.

But the count slowly turned in his favor and on the 10th pitch of the at-bat, O'Neill drew a walk. Pinch hitter Luis Polonia rocketed a single, and Jose Vizcaino singled to load the bases. Knoblauch—who always seemed to contribute at crucial World Series moments in his time with the Yankees—drove a sacrifice fly to left field, tying the game. Three innings later, at 1:04 A.M., Vizcaino came to bat with the bases loaded and two outs. He had been one of seven key players acquired to upgrade the team during the summer, Torre appreciating his ability to put the ball in

Yankee owner George Steinbrenner is framed by the World Series trophy during the Yankees celebration parade at City Hall in New York on October 30, 2000.

handle, the barrel tumbling toward Clemens, who flinched at first. Then Clemens fielded the bat head, turned slightly to his left and whipped the bat sidearm; again it tumbled, across Piazza's path, and the catcher looked up and stared at Clemens, still trying to comprehend what had happened. Clemens tried to continue as if nothing had occurred, asking home plate umpire Charlie Reliford for a new ball. But the Mets' bench emptied, the field filling with anger and confusion. Torre and others restrained John Stearns, the Mets' third-base coach, who shouted at Clemens profanely.

There were no punches thrown, and after the inning, Clemens stopped to talk with Reliford, perhaps realizing he could've been ejected. Then Clemens returned to the Yankees' clubhouse, shaking; he looked for a quiet place to try to calm himself. Clemens would go on to pitch eight scoreless innings, allowing just two hits and no walks and striking out nine. When reporters pressed Mets manager Bobby Valentine after the game to characterize Clemens's bat-throwing incident, Valentine repeatedly mentioned how well Clemens had thrown. But Clemens's performance will always be overshadowed by what occurred in the first inning.

The Yankees had won the first two games and El Duque—undefeated in postseason play— pitched extraordinarily in Game 3, throwing more than 130 pitches before allowing two tiebreaking runs in the eighth inning. That loss ended a string of 14 consecutive World Series victories for the Yankees, a streak that dated back to the Game 2 loss in 1996. Moments before the start of Game 4, Knoblauch predicted to teammates on the bench that if Mets starter Bobby Jones opened the evening with a fastball, Jeter would slug a home run, and that is precisely what happened; one pitch into the game, Jeter had

play, and as he batted against Turk Wendell in the 12th inning, Vizcaino slapped a game-winning single to left field, leaping into the air when he realized the ball was going to fall in.

Clemens pitched Game 2, after nearly a week of buildup before his first rematch with Piazza since the July beaning. Clemens appeared to be in a near frenzy as he took the mound for the first inning, shouting after several pitches, cursing himself after throwing pitches out of the strike zone. He struck out Timo Perez, whiffed Edgardo Alfonzo and with two outs in the first inning, Piazza strolled to the plate, cameras flashing throughout Yankee Stadium.

Clemens whipped a fastball inside to Piazza and the Mets catcher swung. His bat broke at the essentially reversed the momentum established by the Mets the night before.

The Yankees scored single runs in each of the first three innings, before Piazza crushed a two-run homer off Denny Neagle in the bottom of the third. Neagle retired the first two batters in the fifth and was one out from qualifying for a victory, with Piazza coming to bat. Torre stepped out of the dugout, called for Cone from the bullpen and took the ball from an infuriated Neagle, who spent the next few innings raging in the clubhouse about the decision.

Cone had been relegated to the bullpen after a miserable 4–14 season, but Torre asked him, once more, for a big out. Piazza popped up, ending the inning, in what would turn out to be Cone's last playing appearance as a Yankee. Rivera pitched the last two innings, maintaining the one-run advantage, and the Yankees needed one victory to become the first team since the Oakland Athletics of 1972–1974 to win three consecutive championships.

Williams was hitless in his first 14 at-bats in the World Series, but he mashed a home run off Al Leiter in the second inning of Game 5; the Mets countered with two runs in the same inning. Jeter—him again—tied the score with a home run in the sixth, and they played into the late innings like this, implication accompanying every pitch. Leiter was dominant, retiring the Yankees in the seventh, in the eighth, striking out Martinez and O'Neill to open the ninth inning. Leiter's pitch count approached 140, but he had earned the right to finish this game, Valentine thought, and Leiter nearly struck out Posada to close the ninth. But Posada took close pitches and walked, and Scott Brosius singled, bringing utilityman Luis Sojo to the plate.

Sojo rarely played, filling in if an infielder was hurt or Torre needed a defensive replacement in the late innings, sometimes going weeks between at-bats. Torre liked having Sojo for his soft hands, his positive clubhouse presence—he was probably the best-liked member of the team—and his ability to make contact, in spite of one of the worst-looking swings in the majors. Sojo, a right-handed hitter, would often step left with his front foot as he reached with his bat to his right, his rear end jutting out as he struggled to maintain his balance. Sojo looked bad even when he got hits, and Jeter once joked that if he pitched against Sojo, he would throw the ball down the middle of the strike zone.

But Sojo could almost always make contact, and as he walked to the plate to face Leiter—a former teammate from the years when both played for Toronto—he guessed that Leiter was tired and probably would try to challenge him with a fastball. He just wanted to get a pitch to hit and slap at it. Leiter whipped a fastball, as Sojo anticipated, and the Yankees' utilityman bounced a grounder up the middle, the ball rolling like a rock skimming across the top of a lake. Past Leiter, past the lunging middle infielders, into center field. Jay Payton's throw hit Posada as he crossed the plate, and Brosius scored as well, and after Williams gloved Piazza's long drive in the bottom of the ninth, Williams dropped to a knee and crossed himself. Three straight titles.

The cast of players who returned the Yankees to glory in 1996 was mostly gone by 2001. Girardi left after the 1999 season Cone moved on after the 2000 season and even as O'Neill re-signed with the Yankees for the 2001 season, he had decided to retire after one more year. Tino Martinez had one season left on his contract and there was rampant speculation the Yankees would pursue Jason Giambi, the Oakland slugger, for the 2002 season. (They eventually did sign Giambi to a long-term deal.) Rookie Alfonso

Soriano was installed at second base, top hitting prospect Nick Johnson seemed ready to move into the majors and the Yankees signed Drew Henson, a star college quarterback, to an unprecedented six-year deal and made him the

heir apparent at third base, with an estimated time of arrival in 2003.

The 2001 season felt like the last hurrah for a generation of Yankees, as O'Neill acknowledged. Even if the Yankees of 2002 and beyond win championships, he said, they will do so with essentially a different group of players, a different team. Change became more inevitable through the summer, as the Yankees struggled to score runs and appeared more vulnerable than they ever had during the string of titles; by June, Cashman knew the Yankees would undergo a massive off-season overhaul. But the Yankees managed to hold onto first place, because of Clemens, Pettitte, Mike Mussina—who had been signed away from the Baltimore Orioles after the 2000 season—Rivera, Stanton and other key members of the pitching staff. Clemens lost to the Seattle Mariners on May 20 and he would not lose again until September 25. He became the first pitcher in history to open a season with a 20–1 record, and started the All-star Game for the American League. As Clemens moved past other Hall of Fame pitchers in career victories and strikeouts and established a Yankees portfolio, the polite cheers he heard at Yankee Stadium gained warmth. He had become an emotional leader for the Yankees, a standing confirmed on a muggy July day in Detroit.

The Yankees played an extra-inning night game in Philadelphia, and because of an earlier rainout, they had to play a day-night double-header in Detroit the next afternoon. The Yankees arrived at Comerica Park sleep-deprived, Clemens's own face bearing the distinct imprint of a pillow when he walked in at 11

The Yankees are hoping that Alfonso Soriano will be their second baseman for years to come. Here he is greeted by teammates after hitting the game-winning homer in Game 4 of the American League Championship against Seattle in 2001.

Pitchers, from left, Mike Mussina, Andy Pettitte, Roger Clemens and Orlando Hernandez working out at Legends Field in Tampa, Florida.

A.M. He was not scheduled to pitch until the next day, but when Clemens learned that Adrian Hernandez, the scheduled starter for Game 1 of the doubleheader, was unable to pitch because of the flu, Clemens volunteered to fill in. His willingness to take the ball and help the team served as a shot of adrenaline for the team, Martinez and O'Neill said later, and Clemens and the Yankees ground their way to a win, just 17 days shy of Clemens's 39th birthday. The Yankees crushed Boston on September 9, building their lead to 13½ games. Clemens was scheduled to pitch two days later—September 11.

Jorge Posada woke Jeter at home that morning to tell him about the terrorist attacks, and Jeter sat in front of his television for two days, stunned. Stanton heard the horrible news and rushed to pick up his children at school. Knoblauch, a resi-

dent of Manhattan, saw the World Trade Center towers collapse. After waiting two days for a decision on when baseball would resume, Clemens and his wife and a friend drove to their homes in Texas, to be with their children.

The Yankees held their first workout four days after the attacks, most of them unsure of whether they even should be thinking about baseball. But the practices at Yankee Stadium seemed to help them sort through feelings, and gradually the players began to sense they could be of some consolation, in a small way—through their work, they could provide a distraction for a few hours a day, for anyone needing a distraction. They were not comfortable with the idea that they were anointed representatives of their city at this particular time; to suggest that, Brosius said, would imply that they were somehow drawing motivation from unspeakable tragedy. And besides, none of them had experienced the losses that so many others had.

But they were cheered as representatives of New York wherever they played the rest of the year, fans in Chicago and Baltimore and Tampa Bay and elsewhere identifying the Yankees directly with what had occurred in New York. I LOVE NEW YORK, AND EVEN THE YANKEES one sign in Chicago read.

But their offense was floundering and for the first time in Torre's tenure as manager, the Yankees went into the playoffs as a clear underdog. The Oakland Athletics were younger and faster than the Yankees, and had played much better than the Yankees during the year, winning 102 games. Just before the start of the Division Series, Oakland manager Art Howe said the Yankees would have to play a good series to have a chance to beat the Athletics—a bold statement that reflected the seeming decline of the Yankees. And Oakland won the first two games of the best-of-five series, both victories coming in Yankee Stadium. The Yankees' modern-day

The Yankees pause in a moment of silence before they work out for the first time at Yankee Stadium after the terrorist attacks on the United States on September 11, 2001.

Members of the United States Armed Services stretch out a large American flag prior to the start of Game 1 of the American League playoffs in October 2001.

dynasty had never been in this much peril.

Mussina pitched Game 3 against the Athletics' Barry Zito, the two pitchers dominating through the early innings. Jorge Posada ripped a solo homer in the top of the fifth inning and the Yankees had a lead, without much hope for more runs; their offense was simply atrocious. Mussina shut out Oakland into the seventh inning, and retired the first two batters before Jeremy Giambi singled. Terrence Long pulled a double into the right-field corner and Giambi rambled around second and began turning at third, as rightfielder Shane Spencer cut off the ball before it skipped against the wall.

Spencer fired the ball toward home plate strongly, on line, but high over the head of the first cutoff man, Soriano, and the second cutoff man, as well, the ball bounding between home plate and first base. As Posada set himself at home plate and watched the play unfold, Giambi barreled home, and it seemed certain that the ball wasn't going to reach Posada in time. That's when Derek Jeter, who had been stationed near the mound, sprinted into view, catching the ball on a bounce as he ran across the first-base line, and then shoveling it sideways to Posada, like a quarterback pitching a football.

Giambi, moving toward the plate, thought at first he would have to slide, then thought he might have to run over Posada; everything was happening quickly. He ran for the plate, standing, and Posada caught Jeter's throw, swiping blindly toward his left with his glove, tagging the back of Giambi's leg. Out. Inning over. Torre would say afterward that Jeter's improvisation was one of the greatest plays he'd ever seen.

The 1–0 lead held, and the pressure shifted onto the inexperienced Athletics, who wilted. The Yankees routed Oakland in Game 4, 9–2, and Oakland made a handful of mistakes in Game 5.

The Yankees were alive, incredibly, improbably, and they crushed Seattle—which had broken the Yankees' 1998 regular-season victory total—in the championship series, winning the best-of-seven playoff in five games. As they wrecked the Mariners in Game 5, 12–3, the fans in Yankee Stadium chanted and taunted Seattle and their manager, Lou Piniella, through the last four innings. "The one thought that did come to my mind strangely enough is, 'Boy, this city suffered a lot and tonight they let out a lot of emotions,'" said Piniella. "And I felt good for them in that way. And that's a strange thought to come from a manager who is getting his tail kicked."

But the Yankees lost the first two games of the World Series to Arizona aces Curt Schilling and Randy Johnson, and one more time, they were in trouble. Clemens, pitching with a strained hamstring, held the Diamondbacks to one run over seven innings in Game 3 and Brosius dumped a single into left field to score the go-ahead run in the sixth inning. Arizona manager Bob Brenly elected to pitch Schilling on three days' rest in Game 4, and Schilling was masterful, holding the Yankees to a run over seven innings. The Diamondbacks scored twice in the top of the eighth inning, and carried a 3–1 lead into the bottom of the ninth, with closer Byung-Hyun Kim on the mound.

Tino Martinez hadn't seen Kim pitch in person, and before the bottom of the ninth inning, Martinez rushed to the Yankees' video room to examine tape of Kim, to familiarize himself with the pitcher's submarine motion. Paul O'Neill singled with one out and after Bernie Williams struck out, Martinez came to bat; Arizona needed just one out to take a commanding 3 games to 1 lead in the series.

Kim dropped down to begin his delivery, his arm swung through and when Martinez swung, more than 55,000 fans stood to follow the flight of the ball that he crushed. As his home run descended into the stands in right field, Martinez ambled around the bases, his teammates dancing and jumping in front of the home dugout—the first game-tying ninth-inning World Series home run since 1929. The game began on October 31 and at 12:04 A.M., in the first November major-league baseball ever played, Jeter—him again—won the game, ripping a line drive into the right field stands.

Brosius struggled to get to sleep that night, adrenaline coursing through him until close to dawn. He called a night owl friend on the West Coast, and was still stunned by Martinez's home run. "Did you ever see a game like that in your lifetime?" Brosius asked his friend, and the third baseman still wore a grin when he walked into Yankee Stadium before Game 5.

His giddiness was replaced by anxiety soon enough. Mussina allowed back-to-back homers in the fifth inning, and the Diamondbacks led, 2–0, going into the bottom of the ninth. Posada doubled to open the inning, but Kim—back on the mound, with the trust of his manager—retired Spencer and struck out Knoblauch. Brosius was next, representing the last chance for the Yankees, and Kim spun a slider.

But the breaking ball hung, Brosius whipped his bat through the strike zone and as soon as he made contact, Brosius threw his arms into the air, realizing he'd just tied the game with a two-run homer. It had been 72 years since anyone had hit a game-tying home run in the bottom of the ninth inning of a World Series game, and the Yankees did it on back-to-back nights. It didn't seem real; it seemed like destiny. The Yankees

Derek Jeter celebrating after the Yankees eliminated the Oakland A's from the first round of the American League playoffs in October 2001.

won the game in the 12th inning, when Soriano singled home Knoblauch, and despite everything they had gone through, their collective slump, the Yankees led the World Series, 3 games to 2.

To win their fourth consecutive title, they were going to have to beat either Johnson or Schilling in Games 6 and 7, and Johnson and the Diamondbacks crushed Pettitte in Game 6, 15–2. It was Clemens against Schilling in Game 7, the five-time Cy Young Award winner in Clemens—he would get another later in the month, for his pitching in 2001—against someone who considered Clemens a mentor. One run or two might win this game.

No one scored in the first five innings, and when Schilling set down the Yankees in order in the sixth, he had retired 16 consecutive batters. Steve Finley singled to open the sixth for Arizona. Clemens tried to waste a pitch to Danny Bautista, but when Bautista ripped the ball into the left-center field gap, Clemens's whole body sagged; Finley was going to score on the play, and the way the Yankees' offense was going, Clemens knew that one run might be too much.

But the Yankees tied the game in the seventh, Martinez singling home Jeter, and in the top of the eighth inning, Soriano—a rising star of the next generation of Yankees—smashed a home run into the left-field stands. The moment the ball fell amid the devastated fans, Stottlemyre turned to Torre and slapped him on the back. For the last two innings, they had Rivera, who hadn't been beaten in a postseason game in more than four years. He struck out three in the eighth inning, as overwhelming as ever. The Yankees' reserves lined up against their dugout railing as the bottom of the ninth inning began, preparing to storm the field.

Mark Grace singled, and catcher Damian Miller bunted in front of the plate, right back toward Rivera, considered among the best-fielding pitchers in the game. Rivera pounced on the ball, fired toward second base for the force—and the ball sailed into center field. First and second, nobody out. Jay Bell pinch-hit and bunted back to Rivera, who threw to third base for a force, Brosius holding the ball after the catch; instant replay later showed that Brosius probably had time to throw to first base for a double play.

Tony Womack then pulled the ball down the right-field line, and pinch runner Midre Cummings scored and Bell stopped at third, the Arizona fans exploding. The score was tied, still one out. Rivera hit Craig Counsell with a pitch to load the bases, and with Luis Gonzalez coming to bat, Torre elected to move his infielders in, an attempt to pinch off the run. Rivera rarely generated ground ball double plays, anyway, with his cut fastball, usually jamming the hands of left-handed hitters.

Rivera threw a cutter to Gonzalez, who swung and looped the ball toward shortstop, where Jeter raised his gloved hand—and had no chance. The ball fell just over the infield, Bell scored, the Diamondbacks were champions and the Yankees were beaten. Rivera walked off the field impassively, while O'Neill and others lingered in the dugout, stunned. There would be a range of emotions in the Yankees' clubhouse afterward; Jeter seemed to seethe, while others talked about what an incredible series it had been. "We'll be back," Steinbrenner promised.

Several days later, Cashman spoke at an organizational meeting and talked about the needed improvements—an upgrade in on-base percentage, a reemphasis on acquiring strong clubhouse personalities. One of the executives in the room was Gene Michael, and he and other Yankees officials prepared, once again, to construct a championship team.

Each year during spring training could be the year that the next Yankee legend will emerge.

LIST OF ILLUSTRATIONS

stop and Jumpin' Joe Dugan, their third baseman. (Baseball Hall of Fame Library)

36   The 1927 Yankee pitching staff, from left, Bob Shawkey, Joe Giard, Myles Thomas, Urban Shocker, Waite Hoyt, Herb Pennock, Wilcy Moore, Walter Beall, Dutch Ruether and George Pipgras. (Baseball Hall of Fame Library)

37   Joe McCarthy became the team's manager in 1931. He managed the team to eight championships and seven World Championships. (The New York Times)

38   Babe Ruth is congratulated by Lou Gehrig after Ruth hit a homer in the fifth inning of Game 3 of the 1932 World Series in Chicago against the Cubs. The debate continues whether or not Ruth called this homer. (Associated Press)

39   Babe Ruth chopping some wood on his farm. (Times Wide World Photos)

40   Babe Ruth played Santa Claus at a children's charity event at the Hotel Astor in New York in 1947. (Baseball Hall of Fame Library)

41   The bleachers are packed on July 4, 1939, the day Lou Gehrig officially retired. (The New York Times)

42–43   Lou Gehrig decides to take himself out of the lineup on May 1, 1939, after playing in 2,130 consecutive games. He watched his teammates work out before their game against the Tigers in Detroit. (Associated Press)

44   "Today I consider myself the luckiest man on the face of the earth," said Lou Gehrig in a moving farewell speech. (Baseball Hall of Fame Library)

45   Babe Ruth showed up at Lou Gehrig's farewell and threw his arms around Gehrig's neck. (Baseball Hall of Fame Library)

46   Babe Ruth was honored at the 25th anniversary of the opening of Yankee Stadium in 1948. He died two months later. (Nathaniel Fein/New York Herald Tribune)

47   Lou Gehrig and Babe Ruth, the first two stars of the team, remain immortal in the folklore of the team. (Baseball Hall of Fame Library)

PART TWO
GEHRIG–DIMAGGIO (1930s, 40s, 50s)

51   Joe DiMaggio, alias the Yankee Clipper, alias Jolting Joe, alias the Jolter, alias Joe D, flourished as only a baseball icon can for more than six decades. (Baseball Hall of Fame Library)

52   "When he walked into the clubhouse, the lights flickered," Pete Sheehy, the legendary clubhouse man, once said of Joe DiMaggio. (The New York Times)

54   Joe DiMaggio on the family fishing boat in San Francisco with his brother, Mike. Joe preferred baseball to fishing. (Associated Press)

55   Joe DiMaggio batted .398 with 34 homers and 154 runs batted in when he played in the Pacific Coast League in 1935. (Associated Press)

56   The day that Joe DiMaggio arrived at spring training, Lou Gehrig told him, "Nice to have you with us, Joe." (Baseball Hall of Fame Library)

57   Frank Crosetti, Tony Lazzeri and Joe DiMaggio gave their Italian-American fans a lot to cheer for at Yankee Stadium (Times Wide World Photos)

58   Joe DiMaggio would later say that the 1936 team was the best of all the Yankee teams he played for. Some of these Yankees were, from left, Bill Dickey, Lou Gehrig, DiMaggio and Tony Lazzeri. (Times Wide World Photos)

59   Joe DiMaggio batted .346, slugged 46 homers and drove in 167 runs in 1937.

60   Yankees celebrate in the dressing room after defeating the New York Giants, 4-2, in the fifth and final game of the World Series, October 10, 1937. From left are manager Joe McCarthy, owner Jacob Ruppert, Lou Gehrig and Tony Lazzeri. Joe DiMaggio is in the foreground. (Baseball Hall of Fame Library)

61   Joe DiMaggio listening to owner Jacob Ruppert. Joe received a $25,000 salary, with Ruppert's blessing, in 1938. (Baseball Hall of Fame Library)

62   Babe Ruth, left, shakes hands with Joe DiMaggio, at a banquet in New York on January 24, 1938. Sportswriter Bill Corum stood between the two. (Times Wide World Photos)

63   Joe DiMaggio relaxing with Charlie Keller, who joined the team in 1939 and batted .334 with 11 homers. (Baseball Hall of Fame Library)

65   Lefty Gomez working out with his roommate Joe DiMaggio. (Baseball Hall of Fame Library)

66-67   Mayor Fiorello La Guardia of New York presents Joe DiMaggio a gold watch and a citation award as the most valuable baseball player in the American League during the 1939 season. The presentation was made at the Yankee–Cleveland Indians game on August 23, 1940, at Yankee Stadium. (Times Wide World Photos)

69   All the commotion about his hitting streak in 1941 did not faze Joe DiMaggio because he had been through a 61-game streak with the San Francisco Seals, his minor league team. (Associated Press)

70   Joe DiMaggio and Ted Williams of the Red Sox chatting before a doubleheader at Yankee Stadium on July 1, 1941. (Times Wide World Photos)

Mike Burke, Yankee president, stood behind. (The New York Times)

145   Jim "Catfish" Hunter signed to a five-year contract worth $3.35 million in 1974. His contract set a new standard. (Barton Silverman/The New York Times)

146   Billy Martin had been a brawler all his life. He managed the team 1975–1978, 1979, 1983, 1985 and 1988. Here he argues with umpire Jerry Neudecker. (William E. Sauro/The New York Times)

148   Thurman Munson was one of the team's few home-grown stars. Here he is tagging out Dodger Steve Garvey in Game 1 of the 1977 World Series. (Robert Walker/The New York Times)

149   Chris Chambliss is surrounded by fans before he can touch home plate after he hit a ninth-inning, game-winning homer to defeat the Kansas City Royals for the American League Championship on October 14, 1976. (Associated Press)

150   Andy Messersmith speaking at a news conference after meeting with Baseball Commissioner Bowie Kuhn in April 1976. He was challenging baseball's reserve clause. (John Sotomayor/The New York Times)

151   Thurman Munson, left, recommended that the team get Reggie Jackson. (Barton Silverman/The New York Times)

152   New York Yankee manager Billy Martin yells at Reggie Jackson, right, on June 18, 1977, during sixth-inning action in the dugout at Boston. Heated words erupted after Martin took Jackson out of the game. (United Press International)

153   Sparky Lyle being congratulated by Thurman Munson after another save. Lyle was the team's reliever from 1972 to 1978. (Fred Conrad/The New York Times)

154   Reggie Jackson hitting his second of his three home runs against the Dodgers in Game 6 of the 1977 World Series. (Barton Silverman/The New York Times)

156   Thurman Munson, 15, and Chris Chambliss congratulate Reggie Jackson after his third homer against the Dodgers in Game 6 of the 1977 World Series. (Baseball Hall of Fame Library)

157   Babe Ruth crossing home plate after hitting his third home run in Game 4 of the 1928 World Series against the Cardinals. He receives congratulates from Lou Gehrig. (Baseball Hall of Fame Library)

158   Ron Guidry was thinking of quitting the Yankees in 1976. He pitched for the team from 1975 to 1988. He had three 20-game-winning seasons and in 1978 he was 25-3. (Barton Silverman/The New York Times)

159   The Reggie Jackson and Billy Martin soap opera frequently managed to steal the headlines. (Chester Higgins Jr./The New York Times)

160   Graig Nettles makes one of his trademark diving catches. The Yankee captain played with the team from 1973 to 1983. (Associated Press)

161   Bucky Dent, 20, is greeted by teammates after he hit a three-run homer against the Red Sox to help the team win the division championship on October 2, 1978. (Associated Press)

162   Rich "Goose" Gossage was the Yankees' closer from 1978 to 1983. He also played with the team in 1989. (Vic DeLucia/The New York Times)

163   Dick Howser was the new Yankee manager in 1980, the sixth named by George Steinbrenner in his seven years as a principal owner. (The New York Times)

164   Gene Michael, the former shortstop, was named the team's manager in 1982. He has worked with the team in many capacities. (Vic DeLucia/The New York Times)

165   Dave Righetti striking out Wade Boggs of the Red Sox to complete a no-hitter on July 4, 1983. (Barton Silverman/The New York Times)

166   Dave Winfield was productive at bat, on the bases and in the outfield. He was big, amazingly athletic, played hard and was popular with the fans. (Barton Silverman/The New York Times)

167   Dave Collins was assured by George Steinbrenner that he would have a spot in the starting lineup in 1982. He played in only 60 games, went to bat fewer than 400 times and was traded after the season. (Barton Silverman/The New York Times)

168   Lou Piniella scoring for the team. The Twins, Ray Smith took the late throw as Graig Nettles looked on. Piniella played hard for the team from 1974 to 1984. (Jim Wilson/The New York Times)

169   Ed Whitson was ineffective in his starts at Yankee Stadium and became a favorite target for the fans. Here he leaves the mound after allowing five runs on six hits against the Twins in May 1985. (Larry C. Morris/The New York Times)

170   Howard Spira made George Steinbrenner an offer he could not refuse. He was found guilty of attempting to blackmail the Yankees' owner with information about Dave Winfield. (The New York Times)

171   George Steinbrenner returned to baseball in 1993 after missing two and a half years. During that period he named Gene Michael general manager. Michael, who believed in the Yankee farm system, laid the groundwork for the Yankee future. (The New York Times)

PART FIVE
THE MODERN YANKEES

175   Gene Michael speaking at a news conference after he was named general manager and vice president of the

Yankees on August 20, 1990. Stump Merrill, Yankee manager, listened. (G. Paul Burnett/The New York Times)

176   Yankee captain Don Mattingly played for the team from 1982 to 1995. (Larry Morris/The New York Times)

177   Paul O'Neill frequently showed explosive displays of frustration. (Barton Silverman/ The New York Times)

178   Bernie Williams is another example of the team's strong farm system. (Barton Silverman/The New York Times)

179   Andy Pettitte was a 21-game winner in 1996. (Barton Silverman/The New York Times)

180   Joe Torre was not the dynamic hire George Steinbrenner sought. Since Torre was hired he has won four World Championships. (Chang W. Lee/The New York Times)

181   Tino Martinez was the regular first baseman for the team from 1996 to 2001. (Barton Silverman/The New York Times)

182   Joe Girardi played with the team from 1996 to 1999. (Barton Silverman/The New York Times)

183   David Cone came back from an aneurysm to pitch in the last weeks of the 1996 season. (Barton Silverman/The New York Times)

184   Derek Jeter radiated confidence in his rookie season in 1996 and manager Joe Torre was convinced he was going to be a major star. (Vincent Laforet/The New York Times)

185   Jim Leyritz watching his 3-run homer in Game 4 against the Braves in Atlanta in 1996. (Barton Silverman/The New York Times)

186   Reliever John Wetteland, with arm raised, celebrates with teammates after their World Series victory against the Braves in 1996. (G. Paul Burnett/The New York Times)

187   Wade Boggs rides a police horse as he celebrates with fans after the team defeated the Braves for the World Championship at Yankee Stadium in 1996. (Ozier Muhammad/The New York Times)

188   David Wells celebrating his perfect game on May 18, 1998. (Barton Silverman/The New York Times)

189   Orlando "El Duque" Hernandez demonstrates his unusual delivery as he pitches for the team. (Chang W. Lee/The New York Times)

190   Scott Brosius celebrates the team's World Series victory over the Padres in 1998. He was named the series' Most Valuable Player. (Chang W. Lee/The New York Times)

192   The team celebrates their World Series victory over the Braves in 1999. (Chang W. Lee/The New York Times)

193   Derek Jeter celebrates his team's World Series victory over the Braves in 1999 by spraying fans with champagne. (Chang W. Lee/the New York Times)

194   Chuck Knoblauch had a history of throwing problems with the team. (Barton Silverman/The New York Times)

196   Mike Piazza breaking his bat on a foul ball in the first inning as he faced Roger Clemens in the 2000 World Series. (Barton Silverman/The New York Times)

197   Roger Clemens throwing Mike Piazza's broken bat in the direction of the catcher. (Barton Silverman/The New York Times)

198   Luis Sojo, with his unorthodox batting stance, had great ability to make contact with the ball. (Barton Silverman/The New York Times)

199   The Yankees celebrate their 26th World Championship as they defeated the Mets in 2000. (Chang W. Lee/The New York Times)

200   Yankee owner George Steinbrenner is framed by the World Series trophy during the Yankees' celebration parade at City Hall in New York on October 30, 2000.(Vincent Laforet/The New York Times)

202   The Yankees are hoping that Alfonso Soriano will be their second baseman for years to come. Here he is greeted by teammates after hitting the game-winning homer in Game 4 of the American League Championship against Seattle in 2001. (G. Paul Burnett/the New York Times)

203   Pitchers, from left, Mike Mussina, Andy Pettitte, Roger Clemens and Orlando Hernandez working out at Legends Field in Tampa, Florida. (Chang W. Lee/The New York Times)

204   The Yankees pause in a moment of silence before they work out for the first time at Yankee Stadium after the terrorist attacks on the United States on September 11, 2001. (Ray Stubblebine/Reuters)

205   Members of the United States Armed Services stretch out a large American flag prior to the start of Game 1 of the American League playoffs in October 2001. (Chang W. Lee/The New York Times)

207   Derek Jeter celebrating after the Yankees eliminated the Oakland A's from the first round of the American League playoffs in October 2001. (Barton Silverman/The New York Times)

209   Each year during spring training could be the year that the next Yankee legend will emerge. (Barton Silverman/The New York Times)